With thanks to Professor Loraine Saunders, associate lecturer, Liverpool Hope University,
for her expert review of the manuscript.

Marshall Cavendish Benchmark
99 White Plains Rd.
Tarrytown, NY 10591-5502
www.marshallcavendish.us

All Web sites were available and accurate when this book was sent to press.

All quotations are cited in the text. Additional information and sources are included in the
Notes section of this book.

Library of Congress Cataloging-in-Publication Data

Boon, Kevin A.
George Orwell : Animal farm and Nineteen eighty-four /
by Kevin Alexander Boon.
p. cm. — (Writers and their works)
Summary: "A biography of writer George Orwell that describes his era, his
major works—the novels Animal Farm and Nineteen Eighty-Four—his life, and
the legacy of his writing"—Provided by publisher.
Includes bibliographical references and index.
ISBN 978-0-7614-2960-9
1. Orwell, George, 1903-1950. 2. Authors, English—20th century—Biography.
3. Orwell, George, 1903-1950. Animal farm. 4. Orwell, George, 1903-1950. Nineteen eighty-four.
I. Title.
PR6029.R8Z58925 2009
828'.91209—dc22
[B]
2007033743

Photo research by Linda Sykes Picture Research, Hilton Head, SC

The photographs in this book are used by permission and through the courtesy of:
Hulton Archive/Getty Images: cover, 2; Time & Life Picture Archive/Getty Images: 6; Orwell Archive,
Special Collections, University College, London:10, 13, 19, 25, 31, 34, 43, 84; Topfoto/The Image
Works: 12, 113; Heritage Image Partnership: 17; The Granger Collection: 28, 46; Bildarchiv
Preussicher Kulturbesitz/Art Resource, NY: 39; Christopher Cormack/Corbis: 41; Graham
Harrison/Alamy: 44; Peter Coombs/Alamy RF: 54; ©Halas & Batchelor Collection Ltd./
The Bridgeman Art Library: 69; Eleanor Bentall/Corbis: 82; Lebrecht Music and Arts: 88.

Publisher: Michelle Bisson
Art Director: Anahid Hamparian
Series Designer: Sonia Chagbatzanian

Printed in Malaysia
1 3 5 6 4 2

Writers and Their Works

George Orwell:
Animal Farm and
Nineteen Eighty-Four

KEVIN ALEXANDER BOON

mc Marshall Cavendish
Benchmark
New York

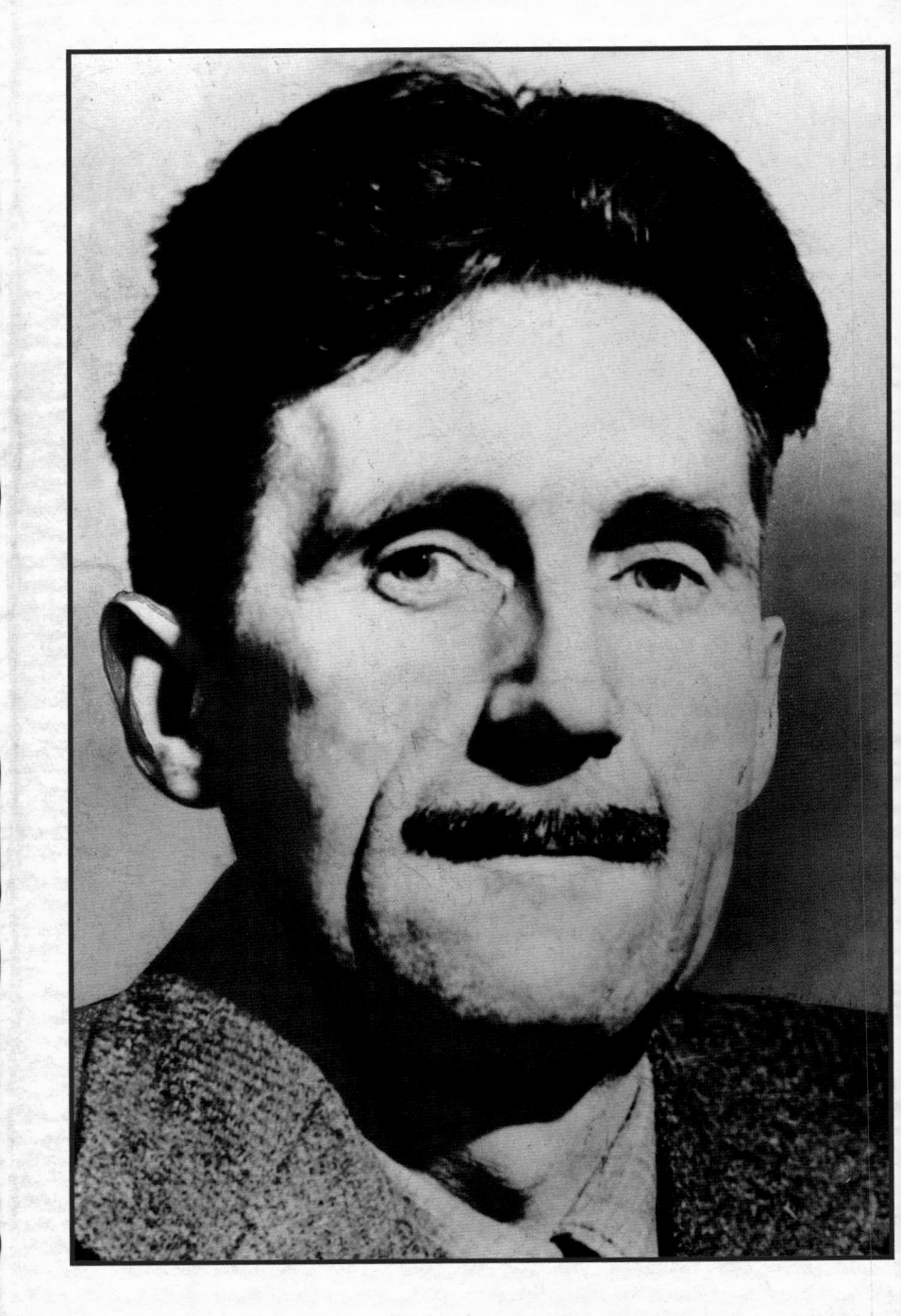

George Orwell:
Animal Farm and Nineteen Eighty-Four

Rebellion!—Old Major, 30

Old Major points out to the animals that their lives are miserable, laborious, and short, that "no animal in England is free," and that the life of an animal is misery and slavery. He explains that the products of their labor are "stolen . . . by human beings," and that "Man is the only real enemy" of the animals, the cause of their "hunger and overwork." He points out that "Man is the only creature that consumes without producing," serving "the interests of no creature except himself." Old Major claims that one day there will be a rebellion and animals will overthrow the tyranny of Man. Work night and day, body and soul, for the overthrow of the human race! That is my message to you, comrades: Rebellion!—Old Major, 30

Introduction

GEORGE ORWELL (Eric Blair) was a skilled essayist, journalist, war correspondent, political commentator, and
novelist. He was an advocate for the working class and a
vocal opponent of totalitarian forms of government. He
wrote on a broad range of subjects, from the coal mines
of northern England to the battlefields of Spain.

Orwell's greatest literary triumphs came during the
last four years of his life, beginning with the success of his
political allegory, *Animal Farm*, a work that criticized the
communism of Stalinist Russia. His second most well-
known work was *Nineteen Eighty-Four*, which he published while on his deathbed. *Nineteen Eighty-Four* is a
dark, futuristic novel that warns of the dangers of totalitarian rule. It is often considered Orwell's masterpiece.

The questions that haunted Orwell throughout his life
involve how people choose to treat one another and how
men of power create systems of government that effectively enslave the poorer members of a culture. Stirred by
the cruelty of British imperialism he experienced as a
young man working in India, the corruption he witnessed
while fighting among communist and socialist forces
against fascism during the Spanish Civil War, the injustice
he chronicled among the working classes in northern
England, and the increasing prevalence of totalitarian
ideas among intellectuals during the first half of the century, Orwell used his writing to counter the rising tide of
oppressive politics, unchecked greed, and abuses of power
that threatened to deprive us all of our humanity.
Although he died in 1950, his writing remains as
relevant today as it was then, and his works continue
to inform new generations about the forces that shape
our world.

Contents

Part I:
The Life of George Orwell

NO ONE WOULD HAVE IMAGINED THAT THE SICKLY THREE-YEAR-OLD IN A SAILOR SUIT WOULD, ONE DAY, SAIL THE WORLD'S SEAS AS A HARDY INTERNATIONAL TRAVELER.

Chapter 1

Citizen Blair

Childhood

GEORGE ORWELL is the literary pseudonym of Eric Arthur Blair, who was born on June 25, 1903, in Motihari, Bengal, when the region was under British rule. Eric's father, Richard Walmesley Blair, was a British official who spent his professional life overseeing opium production in India and its distribution in China for the British East India Company. Opium was legal in India at the time, and the British government made a tidy profit, amounting to "one-sixth of the government's total revenue for India," by selling the narcotic to addicts in Chinese slums. Richard Blair was firmly middle class, loyal to Britain, and content to spend his life in service to the British Crown.

Eric's mother, Ida Mabel (born Limouzin) was eighteen years younger than his father. Eric's older sister, Marjorie Frances, had been born in Bengal in 1898.

In the summer of 1904 the family took leave back in England. When Eric's father returned to India, Eric's mother and the two children remained behind, setting up house at Henley-on-Thames, Oxfordshire, where Ida could raise the family under more genteel circumstances than India offered. Eric's infancy was "punctuated by a series of short illnesses, invariably related to his chest," foreshadowing the health difficulties he would experience throughout his life.

In 1907 Richard Blair returned to England for three months on another leave from his service in India. He and Ida conceived another child, and in April 1908, after

Richard had returned to India, Ida gave birth to Eric's sister, Avril Nora. That same year, Eric enrolled in Sunnylands, an Anglican Convent day school in Henley that his older sister attended.

Eric showed intellectual promise as a child, and Ida began searching for an appropriate preparatory boarding school, one that might eventually lead Eric to earn a place

ERIC BLAIR WAS BORN IN INDIA, BUT HE AND HIS MOTHER AND OLDER SISTER WENT BACK TO ENGLAND SHORTLY THEREAFTER.

THE THIRTEEN-YEAR-OLD ERIC BLAIR (LEFT) POSES WITH (LEFT TO RIGHT) HIS MOTHER, SISTER AVRIL NORA, AND FATHER IN 1916.

in a prestigious public school. Ida's brother, Charles, recommended St. Cyprian's, 60 miles (96.5 kilometers) south of London in Sussex, and in 1911 Eric was enrolled.

In 1912 Eric's father retired from the Indian Civil Service, having risen only to the relatively low rank of sub-deputy opium agent. He rejoined the family in England, but Eric, who had seen little of his father during the early years of his life, was away at St. Cyprian's and only saw his father on holidays.

In the five years that Eric was at St. Cyprian's, he came to despise the school and described it in unflattering terms

in a 1953 essay titled "Such, Such Were the Joys." The targets of much of his scorn were the snobbish students. He recalls one instance in which a Russian boy bragged with "amused contempt" that his father made two hundred times as much money as Eric's father.

Eric particularly disliked the headmaster and his wife, Mr. and Mrs. Wilkes, whom he depicted as greedy and often selfish authority figures. Eric believed that they were unusually harsh to him because he had been accepted into the school at half the usual £180 per year under the presumption that he would excel and bring attention to the school. Despite the ridicule the school eventually faced from its illustrious student, many of Eric's classmates would later claim that Eric's criticism of St. Cyprian's and Mr. and Mrs. Wilkes was exaggerated. One classmate, Walter Christie, said that the young Eric Blair had a "chip on his shoulder" and that St. Cyprian's was "an excellent school . . . where many boys were for the most part happy."

Eric exhibited some literary promise even while at St. Cyprian's. When World War I broke out in 1914, Eric composed a twelve-line poem intended to rally men to England's defense. The poem, titled "Awake! Young Men of England," was published in the *Henley and South Oxfordshire Standard*, a local newspaper. In 1915 he won St. Cyprian's English prize. By 1916 Eric was considered the best poet in the school, and published a second poem in the *Henley and South Oxfordshire Standard*, this time in honor of British war hero Lord Kitchener, who died when the HMS *Hampshire* hit a German mine on its way to Russia. Cyril Connelly, Eric's best friend at St. Cyprian's, would later claim that Eric was the only "intellectual" at the school, "one of those boys who seem born old."

Eric performed well during his last years at St. Cyprian's, but he was content to leave the school behind at the end of 1916. His life up to this point had instilled in him a sense of inferiority, despite his occasional

successes. Biographer D. J. Taylor characterizes Orwell as a man "obsessed by the idea of failure." Scholar Peter Davison points out that "until he left St. Cyprian's, Orwell's conditioning . . . was such as to make him feel, fairly or not, that he was, if not unloved, passed over; easily 'parked out'; inferior; and, inevitably, a failure."

A King's Scholar at Eton

In 1917, after one term at Wellington College, he entered Eton College as a King's Scholar (an academic scholarship program established by King Henry VI, who founded the college in 1440). At Eton Eric spent much of his time reading. He was particularly fond of the works of Jack London, H. G. Wells, D. H. Lawrence, and George Bernard Shaw. He would later praise Shaw's work, claiming that Shaw was especially good when he attacked "the humbug of puritanical monied [sic] society."

Eric's status as a King's Scholar placed him among seventy intellectually elite students in a class of one thousand socially privileged boys. Eric's academic performance at Eton was not exceptional, but he was remembered by his classmates as an observant boy who "followed his own path."

Eric's growing literary talent was put to use to express his increasing interest in Jacintha Buddicom, an older girl he first met, along with her sister, Guinever, and brother, Prosper, in the summer of 1914. The four became friends, and Eric often spent school holidays with the Buddicom children. As he matured, Eric became enamored of Jacintha. In 1918 he sent her a love poem called "The Pagan," which includes the passage:

> So here are you, and here am I,
> Where we may thank our gods to be;
> Above the earth, beneath the sky,
> Naked souls alive and free.

The poem, which was inspired by the poetry of A. E. Housman, reveals Eric's burgeoning interest in romance. The sonnet he wrote for her two months later further exposes his romantic interest in Jacintha and, amid references to Shakespeare's *Romeo and Juliet*, contains the following quatrain:

> Our minds are married, but we are too young
> For wedlock by the customs of this age
> When parent homes pen each in separate cage
> And only supper-earning songs are sung.

Although Jacintha never returned Eric's romantic interest, she inspired his first major love.

In the summer of 1920 Eric had his first experience with "tramping." He missed a train connection on his way to join his family in Looe, England, for the remainder of the holiday and was forced to make his own way in Plymouth. He was dressed in uniform, having just come from Officer Training Corps, and only had seven pence (equivalent to a few cents). He bought some rolls for dinner and spent the night sleeping behind a bush in a farmer's field. Eric found the experience liberating. The freedom of being on his own excited his imagination and filled him with a sense of adventure.

At the end of 1921 Eric's father and mother retired to Southwold, Suffolk, to live out the remainder of their lives. Eric joined them there after completing his studies at Eton, having grown to a height of 6 feet 3 inches.

India

For six months during 1922 Eric Blair lived in Southwold with his parents. Blair wanted to continue his education at university, but his grades were too low to secure a scholarship. Furthermore, his father strongly objected. Indian service appealed to Blair's father as a sensible choice for a young man, having made that choice for himself.

So, Blair studied for the entrance exams in order to acquire a well-paid position in the Indian Imperial Police while he waited to turn nineteen, the minimum age required for service.

By joining the Indian police, Blair would be committing himself to a career that would place him in India for long periods of time. Growing up, Blair thought that he

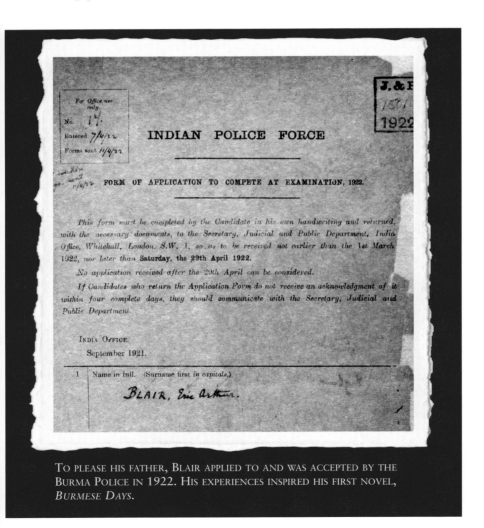

TO PLEASE HIS FATHER, BLAIR APPLIED TO AND WAS ACCEPTED BY THE BURMA POLICE IN 1922. HIS EXPERIENCES INSPIRED HIS FIRST NOVEL, *BURMESE DAYS*.

might like to be a writer, but he knew that his father would not approve of his profession. Blair barely passed the horse-riding test required for service, but once he was accepted into the Indian police he showed a talent for learning languages, mastering Burmese, Hindustani, and Shaw-Karen.

He sailed for Burma in October 1922 and arrived at Mandalay in November, where he assumed the position of probationary assistant superintendent of police. On November 29 he began nine months of training in police procedure, law, and languages.

In 1922 the British Empire was at its height, controlling one-fourth of the world. Much of this land was ruled by the British Crown, but not populated with British subjects. The lands were exploited for their natural resources or their strategic locations. In Burma (now called the Union of Myanmar) the ruling British considered themselves superior to the indigenous people of the region and generally did not mix with them. Decades of colonial oppression had left much of the Burmese population bitter. When Blair arrived, the country had just undergone "serious political disturbance," and hostility toward the ruling authority was high. The country was experiencing a crime wave.

Blair describes Mandalay as a "disagreeable town—it is dusty and intolerably hot, and it is said to have five main products all beginning with P, namely, pagodas, pariahs, pigs, priests and prostitutes." British subjects living in India tried to maintain British social graces and established for themselves a life separate from Burmese culture. Yet Blair was uncomfortable with his social role as a British member of the Indian Police and often kept to himself. He was, however, fascinated by the lower classes and those who lived on the periphery of polite British society. In one instance he befriended Captain H. R. Robinson, a former military police officer who had

Eric Blair (back row, third from left) stands tall in a group photo taken at the police mess in Mandalay, Burma, in 1923.

become addicted to opium, was dismissed from service, and now lived on the outskirts of society.

The longer Blair stayed in India, the more he disliked the system of imperial rule. He later explained: "I was in the Indian Police five years, and by the end of that time I hated the imperialism I was serving with a bitterness which I probably cannot make clear. In the free air of England that kind of thing is not fully intelligible. In order to hate imperialism you have got to be part of it. Seen from the outside the British rule in India appears—indeed, it *is*—benevolent and even necessary. . . . But it is not possible to be a part of such a system without recognizing it

as an unjustifiable tyranny." Early observations such as these helped shape Blair's political ideas and would ultimately influence the course of his writings as George Orwell.

While stationed in Katha, Blair caught dengue fever, a tropical disease that further weakened his health. Biographer Michael Shelden claims that during his recovery, Blair finally accepted that Indian service was not the career for him. In June Blair was granted an eight-month leave for medical reasons. In July he began the two-month-long voyage back to England. Scholar Douglas Kerr argues that Blair returned from colonial Burma with "a simple and serviceable idea of how society worked: one kind of people rather nervously held power over another kind." Kerr further notes that "in the East the powerless greatly outnumbered the powerful, and there was a visible racial difference between them; and this difference was held to be the justification for the privilege of one kind over the other."

During a stopover in Marseilles, France, Blair witnessed a demonstration against the American imprisonment of Sacco and Vanzetti, two Italian immigrants accused of the robbery and murder of a shoe factory employee. The two men were anarchists, but many felt they were innocent men who had been railroaded by prejudice against Italians, immigrants, and people with unpopular political beliefs. Blair was impressed with the ability of the French to engage in civil disobedience in opposition to injustice.

In August 1927 Blair arrived at his parent's house in Southwold, having spent five years in India.

New Directions
On vacation in Polperro, Blair told the family that he was resigning his commission and would not be returning to India. Blair's father could not imagine why anyone would

abandon such an important and well-paid position. A friend of Blair's later affirmed that Blair's father was "very disappointed. And looked upon him [Blair] as a sort of failure."

Blair could have remained on leave at full pay until March, but decided instead to resign his post effective January 1928, thus forfeiting more than two months' pay in order to receive his freedom sooner.

He lived meagerly on money he had saved from his service in Burma while he tried to launch a new career as a writer. He said of the experience, "I felt that I had got to escape not merely from imperialism but from every form of man's dominion over man. . . . Failure seemed to me to be the only virtue. Every suspicion of self-advancement, even to 'succeed' in life to the extent of making a few hundreds a year, seemed to me spiritually ugly, a species of bullying."

He rented an inexpensive, unheated room in London, where he began writing short stories and poetry. His health was not good and working in the unfavorable conditions of his cheap lodging, where he often had to warm his hands by candle flame to continue writing, could not have been good for him, but Blair seldom complained.

Fascinated by the lives of the poor, Blair began dressing as a tramp and frequenting the shadier sections of London, mixing with the lowest classes—"stevedores, sailors, and unemployed laborers." Much of what he learned from these tramping expeditions would find its way into his writing later in life.

In April 1928 Blair moved to Paris looking for artistic inspiration. In the 1920s, Paris was *the* place to be for aspiring writers, and many writers were drawn to the city, including Ernest Hemingway, F. Scott Fitzgerald, James Joyce, and Ezra Pound. Blair worked diligently to establish himself, but with meager success, though he produced a lot of work, including two novels (an early draft of

Burmese Days and a lost manuscript) and early drafts of the nonfiction book *Down and Out in Paris and London.* The first work Blair published in his new career was the article "La Censure en Angleterre" ("Censorship in England"), which he sold to the literary journal *Le Monde*, in October 1928. In December he began selling pieces to *Progrés Civique* and *GK's Weekly*, and heard from literary agent L. I. Bailey. Bailey had been contacted by Blair's Aunt Nellie, who took a great interest in her nephew's writing. Bailey asked to see some of his short stories, and tried to sell some of Blair's work. He was unsuccessful and quickly gave up on Blair.

Blair's health remained poor and at one point he began coughing up blood. He spent several weeks in the public ward of Hôpital Cochin, where he saw that health care was administered to the poor with indifference.

Despite a smattering of publications, Blair's financial situation in Paris was often desperate. At times he went without food and was forced at one point to take a job working thirteen hours a day as a dishwasher. Once, he and a Russian friend pawned their overcoats to get money for food. By the close of 1929 he'd had enough. He borrowed a little money and returned to England, where he rejoined his family in Southwold just before Christmas. There, he discovered that *Adelphi*, a magazine edited by Max Plowman and Sir Richard Rees, was interested in publishing one of Blair's articles on tramps. This publication marked the beginning of Blair's ongoing literary relationship with *Adelphi* (primarily writing reviews) and his long friendship with both Plowman and Rees.

Blair remained in his parents' house, though, according to his younger sister, Avril, he "loathed Southwold." A month after arriving, Blair began traveling to Walberswick, where he tutored a boy with disabilities, whom he later described as a "congenital imbecile." His social life was limited, but he did befriend a vicar's daughter named Brenda Salkeld, who worked at St. Felix's

School for Girls. The two got on well, but Brenda, by her own admission, never loved Blair. For several months in the 1930s he tried to convince her to marry him, but she refused and he eventually stopped asking. The two remained friends.

From March to June of 1930 Blair visited his older sister, Marjorie, and her husband in Yorkshire. There he worked on a book (that he would finish in October) about his days tramping in London and Paris. The original title was *A Scullion's Diary*. In March he found additional work tutoring the three sons of Mr. and Mrs. C. R. Peters. In August, back in Southwold, he met Francis and Mabel Fierz, a steel manufacturer and his wife from London. Mabel knew Max Plowman and helped cement Blair and Plowman's friendship.

Blair continued his tramping expeditions, dressing in old clothes, hanging out with beggars and petty thieves and, for a time, working alongside them in the hop fields. Toward the end of 1930, he sent an early version of what would become *Down and Out in Paris and London* to the Jonathan Cape publishing house. Cape rejected the manuscript. Blair sought help from Sir Richard Rees, who recommended him to T. S. Eliot. Blair contacted Eliot, an editorial director at Faber and Faber, but instead of submitting his manuscript, he offered to translate a French novel by Jacques Roberti.

In December Blair finally sent his tramping manuscript to Eliot at Faber and Faber and contacted Leonard Moore, a literary agent with whom Mabel Fierz had put him in touch. Eliot turned down the manuscript, but Blair had made an important contact in Moore. On Mabel's recommendation Blair took his manuscript (now called *Days in Paris and London*) to Moore's office in 1932.

In April Blair accepted a full-time teaching position at The Hawthorns, a private boys' school, and Leonard Moore agreed to represent Blair's manuscript. Blair was pleased about Moore's offer, but told him that he was

"not proud" of the manuscript and wanted to publish it under a pseudonym. Moore quickly arranged for the book to be published by Victor Gollancz with the understanding that Blair would make some revisions to shield the publisher from potential libel suits. Blair made the requested changes, and in November he sent Moore a list of four possible pseudonyms—P. S. Burton, Kenneth Miles, H. Lewis Allways, and George Orwell, adding that he preferred Orwell.

Eric Blair Becomes George Orwell

Gollancz suggested that *Down and Out in Paris and London* be published under the name "X," but Eric Blair thought he should use a pseudonym that he might use again if the book was successful. Blair had created the name George Orwell by combining the "quintessentially English name" George with the name of a river (the River Orwell) that flows south of Suffolk.

Down and Out in Paris and London was published in January 1933. Orwell only received a £40 (equivalent to about $160 in 1933) advance for the book and continued teaching at The Hawthorns, but he was pleased by the generally good reception the book received. Novelist Compton Mackenzie called the book "a clearly genuine human document which at the same time is written with so much simple force that in spite of the squalor and degradation thus unfolded, the result is curiously beautiful with the beauty of an accomplished etching on copper." Writer and critic J. B. Priestley called it "uncommonly good reading. An excellent book and a valuable social document." Herbert Gorman, who reviewed the American edition of the book (published by Harper & Brothers) for the *New York Times*, disagreed with Mackenzie's claim that the book was "beautiful," but admitted that the book was "vivid and compact with a vigor that makes the reader realize that Mr. Orwell is writing with some indignation."

ERIC BLAIR BECAME GEORGE ORWELL WITH THE PUBLICATION OF HIS
FIRST BOOK, *DOWN AND OUT IN PARIS AND LONDON*.

Encouraged by the reception of his first book, Orwell worked diligently on his next—a novel drawing from his experiences in Burma. Meanwhile, he had left The Hawthorns and taken a position teaching French at Frays College, which he hoped would free up more time for writing. It did not. Nevertheless, he managed to complete his novel, *Burmese Days*, by December.

That same month, Orwell's health suffered another blow. While riding his motorcycle in a rainstorm, he contracted pneumonia and was admitted to Uxbridge Hospital. His illness was serious enough that some thought he would not survive. He was released from the hospital in January 1934, after which he resigned his position at Frays for health reasons and returned to Southwold.

Orwell was beset with more bad news when he learned that two publishers—Gollancz, who had published Orwell's first book, and Heinemann—had rejected

Burmese Days. Once again, they were concerned about possible libel suits. Orwell was reassured when the American publisher, Harper & Brothers, agreed to publish the book if Orwell made a few changes.

In October 1934 Orwell completed his next novel, *A Clergyman's Daughter*, while recovering his health in Southwold. After delivering the book to his agent, Leonard Moore, Orwell took a part-time job working at Booklovers' Corner, a bookstore in London. *Burmese Days* appeared in American bookstores, and Harper & Brothers paid Orwell a £50 advance (about $3,800 today), which helped support him in London.

At the start of 1935 Orwell received good news. Gollancz had agreed to publish *A Clergyman's Daughter* if, as before, Orwell would make some changes to avoid libel. They also wanted to take another look at *Burmese Days* now that Harper & Brothers had published the book in America without attracting any lawsuits. In March Gollancz published *A Clergyman's Daughter*, and in June they published the British version of *Burmese Days*.

Despite Orwell's frequent disappointment with his own work, *A Clergyman's Daughter* received a good review in the *Times Literary Supplement*, which claimed that Orwell's "first novel" bore out the "promise" evident in *Down and Out in Paris and London*. Other reviewers, however, were slightly less positive. Peter Quennell's review in the *New Statesman* said the novel was "ambitious yet not entirely successful," and L. P. Hartley's review in the *Observer* said the novel's thesis was "neither new nor convincing." Nevertheless, Hartley granted that Orwell's handling of the subject was "sure and bold" and that the dialogue was "often brilliant."

The review of *Burmese Days* that appeared in the *Times Literary Supplement* two months later took issue with Orwell's harsh portrayal of "English superiors" in India, but was still, for the most part, favorable.

Orwell was normally shy and overcritical of his work, but in view of his recent successes as a writer, he decided to celebrate by throwing a small party. He invited Rees and a few other friends and asked his landlady to round out the guest list by asking some of her friends to come. She invited several students and teachers from the Psychology Department of University College. Eileen Maud O'Shaughnessy was among the guests. Eileen was intelligent, well read, and attractive. Orwell was instantly interested and spent much of the evening talking with her. Afterward, he remarked that Eileen was "the sort of girl I'd like to marry." Shortly after that, he proposed marriage, but she was working on her degree in psychology, with the goal of becoming an educational psychologist, and stalled him until she finished her degree.

Throughout the summer Orwell worked diligently on his next novel, *Keep the Aspidistra Flying*, acutely aware of the rising threat Germany posed to England. Having received no libel suits from Orwell's previous two novels, Gollancz was eager to have a copy of the new novel by the end of the year. In January 1936 Orwell delivered the manuscript, and Gollancz offered him a commission to write about "unemployment and living conditions in the north of England." Orwell accepted, quit his job at the bookstore, gave up his apartment, and traveled north.

The Road to Wigan Pier and Spain

Orwell spent two months in northern England researching his next book for Gollancz. Scholar Peter Davison claims that this period (coupled with Orwell's later six months in Spain) represented "the turning-point in Orwell's political education, his development as a writer, and his health."

Orwell's latest adventure among Britain's poor led him to Wigan, a town that was suffering from a 25 to 33 percent unemployment rate in the wake of an economic depression that had begun in 1929. Orwell visited with working-class families, miners, and Labour activists, and

UNEMPLOYED COAL MINERS SUCH AS THIS MAN PHOTOGRAPHED AT WIGAN IN THE 1930S INSPIRED *THE ROAD TO WIGAN PIER*.

walked the canal looking for Wigan Pier, a place that turned out to be an old joke made about a now nonexistent wooden jetty. In Wigan (and in a great deal of the north) Orwell saw a "fearful landscape of slagheaps and blackened chimneys and . . . [noted] the rats—weak with hunger, he assumed—faltering through the snow."

While collecting information for *The Road to Wigan Pier*, Orwell was forced to make revisions to *Keep the Aspidistra Flying* at the request of Norman Collins, deputy chairman at Gollancz. Once again the issues were primarily related to the highly biographical nature of the novel and the possibility that some party might sue the publisher for libel. The book was published in Britain in April 1936. Orwell's American publisher decided against publication based on the poor sales of *A Clergyman's Daughter*.

Some of the impoverished living conditions that Orwell encountered while researching *The Road to Wigan Pier* reminded him of "the worst slums in Burma." In "George Orwell's Literary Studies of Poverty in England," scholar Gordon B. Beadle reminds us of Orwell's own claim that his "descent into the 'lowest of the low' was motivated by an irrational desire to expiate an accumulated sense of guilt that he had come to feel as a result of having served the 'evil despotism' of imperialism as a policeman in Burma."

In April 1936 Orwell returned from the north and rented a former village shop 30 miles (48.3 km) north of London in Wallington, Hertfordshire. *Keep the Aspidistra Flying* was published. It sold poorly and received generally bad reviews, although the *Times Literary Supplement* review said the novel was "worth reading." In May Orwell began writing *The Road to Wigan Pier*. In June he and Eileen O'Shaughnessy married.

Richard Wollheim claims that *The Road to Wigan Pier* poses the question, "What is it really to be a

Socialist?" Most agree that "Orwell's two months in the north pushed him closer to socialism," a movement struggling to counter fascism's threat to democracy and the working class. In 1936 fascism had taken root in Germany under the leadership of Adolf Hitler and was threatening to establish itself in France and Spain. Socialists and communists joined forces in an attempt to halt the spread of fascism. The Popular Front, as the coalition was called, successfully blocked fascist attempts to seize power in France, but failed in Spain, where right-wing military forces led by General Francisco Franco thrust the country into civil war in July 1936.

In November Orwell decided to join the socialist forces in Spain as soon as revisions of *The Road to Wigan Pier* were completed. In December he sent the finished manuscript to Leonard Moore and left England, arriving in Barcelona, Spain, on December 26. He carried a letter of introduction to Independent Labour Party (ILP) representative John McNair. McNair was familiar with Orwell's work and enlisted Orwell in the Partido Obrero de Unificación Marxista (POUM), the Worker's Party of Marxist Unification. Orwell thought that his weak lungs might keep him out of battle, but among the poorly prepared ranks he encountered, the drill training he had received while at St. Cyprian's was valuable, and he was charged with leading drills at the Lenin Barracks, where he was housed.

Orwell expected to find a unified sense of purpose among the various left-wing factions fighting fascism in Spain. He was disappointed to learn that the anarchists, communists, and other groups on the left did not get along. In *Homage to Catalonia* Orwell pointed out that communism and anarchism are philosophically "poles apart," and defined the POUM political position as one that claims, "It is nonsense to talk of opposing Fascism by bourgeois 'democracy.' Bourgeois 'democracy' is only

ORWELL WAS IDEALISTIC WHEN HE JOINED THE SPANISH LOYALISTS DURING THE SPANISH CIVIL WAR, BUT HIS VIEWS ON COMMUNISM QUICKLY SOURED.

another name for capitalism, and so is Fascism; to fight against Fascism on behalf of 'democracy' is to fight against one form of capitalism on behalf of a second which is liable to turn into the first at any moment."

In January 1937 Orwell was sent to the front near the town of Alcubierre, where his skill with languages earned him a promotion to corporal. While Orwell endured the brutal cold and "a little shell-fire," which he described as "extraordinarily ineffectual," Eileen took a volunteer position working for John McNair and the ILP in Barcelona. In March she visited Orwell on the front line at Huesca, where he had been transferred.

Orwell spent 115 days on the front. While the cold and lice made his time there uncomfortable, his only

significant injury was an infected cut to his hand, for which he spent a few days in hospital. He received his first leave in April 1937 and joined Eileen in Barcelona, where he filed for a discharge from POUM in order to join the International Brigade, a group made up of volunteers from fifty-three countries who believed in their antifascist cause. The International Brigade was engaging Franco's Spanish Nationalist forces, German Nazis, and Italian Fascists at the Madrid front. Orwell's desire to join the International Brigade was prompted by his hope of seeing more military action.

In May four days of riots broke out in Barcelona, and Orwell spent three days guarding POUM headquarters from the roof of the Poliorama Theatre. Orwell soon lost interest in joining the International Brigade because it had fallen under communist control, and Russian Communist leader Stalin was, Orwell felt, stirring distrust among left-wing groups. Orwell, now a second lieutenant, returned to the front at Huesca on May 10. Ten days later, around 5 a.m., as the sun was rising, he received a near fatal wound to his neck from a fascist sniper. He describes the experience in *Homage to Catalonia*:

> It was the sensation of being *at the centre* of an explosion. There seemed to be a loud bang and a blinding flash of light all round me, and I felt a tremendous shock—no pain, only a violent shock, such as you get from an electric terminal; with it a sense of utter weakness, a feeling of being stricken and shriveled up to nothing. The sand-bags in front of me receded into immense distance. I fancy you would feel much the same if you were struck by lightning. I knew immediately that I was hit, but because of the seeming bang and flash I thought it was a rifle nearby that had gone off accidentally and shot me. All this happened in a

space of time much less than a second. The next moment my knees crumpled up and I was falling, my head hitting the ground with a violent bang which, to my relief, did not hurt. I had a numb, dazed feeling, a consciousness of being very badly hurt, but no pain in the ordinary sense.

Orwell was removed from the front, sent to a hospital in Lerida, and then transferred to a sanatorium in Tibidabo where he quickly regained his ability to speak. Orwell knew that his wound had left him unfit for service and that he would have to leave Spain. Meanwhile, Stalin's forces became more aggressive against the POUM, which was affiliated with Soviet politician Leon Trotsky. In June the POUM newspaper (La Batalla) was banned and the POUM party was outlawed. Orwell and Eileen were both falsely labeled "known Trotskyists" and, if caught, would have been arrested and possibly shot. Their mutual friend, Georges Kopp, was arrested. Unable to secure Kopp's release, the Orwells and John McNair narrowly escaped Barcelona by train.

After a brief and unsuccessful holiday in Banyuls-sur-Mer, France, they returned to England. In 1938 Orwell completed *Homage to Catalonia*, recounting his experiences in Spain. Although he finished the book in January, it was not published until April, partly because it was critical of Stalinist Russia, which was seen by many as an ally in the fight against fascism and thereby above criticism.

Declining Health, a Trip to Morocco, and Another War

In March Orwell began coughing up blood and was taken to Preston Hall Sanatorium in Kent. No evidence of tuberculosis was found, but it was still suspected and Orwell spent five and a half months recuperating from his illness in the sanatorium. There, Orwell planned his next novel, which was to be called *Coming Up for Air*.

ORWELL'S FIRST WIFE, EILEEN MAUD O'SHAUGHNESSY, JOINED HIM IN THE FIGHT AGAINST THE FASCISTS IN SPAIN AND, WITH HIM, WAS MIS-LABELED A TROTSKYIST.

Orwell's doctors recommended a warmer climate, and in September the Orwells traveled to Marrakech in French Morocco with money borrowed from L. H. Myers, the novelist. In the summer Orwell officially joined the Independent Labour Party (ILP), having learned the importance of active involvement in the socialist movement from his time in Spain. But Orwell only remained with the ILP for a short time. The ILP opposed war, but Hitler and the German Nazi Party had already taken over Austria and occupied Sudetenland in western Czechoslovakia and had their sights on Europe. Orwell felt that an antiwar stance in light of the fascist threat to England was unconscionable. In January 1939 Orwell finished a draft of his next novel, *Coming Up for Air*, while Europe moved closer to war.

Orwell disliked Morocco, referring to it as "a beastly dull country, no forests and literally no wild animals, and the people anywhere near a big town utterly debauched by the tourist racket and their poverty combined, which turn them into a race of beggars and curio-sellers." Particularly disturbing was the fact that the French who occupied the country lived well while the Arab population suffered in poverty.

In March Germany invaded the rest of Czechoslovakia, and pressure to enter into war with Germany increased in England and France. The Orwells returned to England, where Orwell delivered the completed manuscript of *Coming Up for Air* to Gollancz before visiting his ailing father in Southwold, who died of intestinal cancer on June 28.

In April the Orwells returned to their home in Wallington, where Orwell began work on a long essay about the writing of Charles Dickens. *Coming Up for Air* was published in June. It sold much better than *Homage to Catalonia* and a second printing was ordered during its first month. Some, however, argue that Orwell had yet to

realize his potential as a novelist. D. J. Taylor expresses this position in his biography of Orwell: "As a novelist, Orwell scarcely begins to exist. His early books—from *Burmese Days*, say, to *Coming Up for Air*—are derivative . . . and something worse than this: projections of his own self-pity, in which the writer's life is used, quite unmediated, for the purposes of art. The results are not only clumsily executed but lack all artistic conviction."

In August Germany signed a nonaggression pact with Russia. On September 1 Germany invaded Poland, and two days later Britain declared war against Germany, marking the start of World War II. Despite his socialist views and his opposition to capitalist imperialism, Orwell's loyalty to England stirred his support for Britain's fight against Hitler's fascist rule. Although Orwell continued to write reviews and articles, for the most part, he put his career on hold while he considered ways to serve the British war effort.

In the spring of 1940 Germany invaded Normandy. It was only a matter of time before the war reached British soil. Orwell had remained alone in Wallington while Eileen stayed in London, but in May he moved to a top-floor flat in London to be closer to her and the British fight. In June Germany defeated the French. During the conflict, Eileen's brother was killed serving with the British Expeditionary Forces in France. Eileen idolized her brother and was devastated by the news. Meanwhile, Orwell joined the Home Guard and prepared for the inevitable German assault against Britain. He helped train recruits for street fighting and studied bomb making, but he and other British volunteers never had an opportunity to engage the German forces. In early September Germany began the Blitz, a concentrated series of bombing attacks that resulted in the deaths of more than 43,000 British subjects and the destruction of a million homes.

In 1941 Orwell began to write a series of articles for the influential *Partisan Review*. Orwell would contribute his "London Letter" articles for the next five years. According to one biographer, Orwell's most important publication in 1941 was *The Lion and the Unicorn*, the first volume in a series published by Secker and Warburg, intended to "serve as an arsenal for the manufacture of mental and spiritual weapons needed for the crusade against Nazism." The work established Orwell as an important advocate for democratic socialism.

On June 22 Germany attacked Russia, violating the nonaggression pact they had signed, and the USSR became a British ally.

In August Orwell accepted a position with the British Broadcasting Company (BBC) as a radio broadcaster for the Indian Section of the Eastern Service, which created pro-British programs to be broadcast in India. Orwell found the system overly bureaucratic and objected to the censorship imposed on him by the British Ministry of Information. Nevertheless, he viewed the position as a way to contribute to the war effort. In the spring of 1942 Eileen began working for the Ministry of Food, where she managed "The Kitchen Front," a Home Service broadcast offering culinary strategies for dealing with wartime shortages.

In March 1943 Orwell's mother died of heart failure. Orwell never commented on her death, but biographer Michael Shelden correlates the death of Orwell's mother with Orwell's sudden interest in having children. Orwell was apparently sterile, so the couple would have to adopt. At first Eileen resisted, worried that she could not handle the strain of caring for an infant, but Orwell persisted, and she eventually acquiesced.

In June the Orwells adopted a newborn boy through the office of Gwen O'Shaughnessy, a medical doctor who

often delivered unwanted children born from wartime romances. The boy was named Richard Horatio Blair.

Orwell worked to produce quality programming, but he realized that only one in every two thousand Indians had a radio capable of receiving the broadcasts and that very few of the people the broadcasts were designed to influence ever heard them. He considered his efforts futile and frustrating. Despite these reservations, Orwell remained with the BBC until November 1943, the same month he began work on what would become one of his most well-known and most successful books—*Animal Farm*. In December he began writing a weekly column titled "As I Please" for the *London Tribune*.

With Eileen's encouragement, Orwell completed *Animal Farm* in February 1944. Orwell's intention with the book was "to make a forceful attack, in an imaginative way, on the sustaining myths of Soviet Communism." He did not suspect that it would be the work that launched him as a major literary figure.

In March Gollancz asked to see the manuscript, but rejected it in April. Most people saw the USSR as an important ally in Britain's struggle against Germany, and Gollancz was not comfortable publishing a book that criticized Soviet communism.

Toward the end of June, a V-1 flying bomb exploded near the Orwells' apartment, causing the roof to collapse. Fortunately, Orwell managed to recover his only copy of *Animal Farm* from the refuse. He sent the rumpled manuscript to T. S. Eliot at Faber and Faber, but Eliot, too, rejected the manuscript.

In July Orwell sent *Animal Farm* to Fredric Warburg at Secker and Warburg, and in August Warburg offered to publish the book. Warburg explained to Orwell that because of paper shortages caused by the war, Secker and Warburg could not publish the book for another year.

ORWELL BECAME A PROUD FATHER IN 1943. HE HOLDS HIS SON,
RICHARD HORATIO BLAIR, IN HIS ARMS.

In February 1945 Orwell accepted an offer to become a war correspondent for the *Observer*. In March he traveled to the Hotel Scribe in Paris. In his absence Eileen learned that she had uterine tumors and would have to undergo a hysterectomy. She entered the hospital in Newcastle on March 22. On March 29, the day of her operation, she had a bad reaction to anesthesia and died of heart failure. Orwell received news of her death by telegram the following day and made immediate plans to return to England.

After Eileen's funeral, Orwell returned to his position as a correspondent and traveled to Germany, hoping that his journalism would help ease his grief. He was shocked by the wide-sweeping devastation he saw in Germany, and surprised that the war had not led to socialism or fascism for the British people.

He was back in England by June, where he hired Susan Watson, a twenty-eight-year-old divorced mother of one daughter, as a live-in housekeeper and caretaker for Richard.

On August 6 an atomic bomb was dropped on Hiroshima. Three days later, on August 9 another was dropped on Nagasaki. Japan surrendered to the United States on August 14, ending World War II. Three days later *Animal Farm* was published.

The Final Years

Toward the end of 1945, Orwell met Sonia Brownell at a dinner party. He was attracted to her strength and beauty, but her initial impression was that he was "a cold Englishman." She would become his second wife, but it would take quite some time to bring the two together.

Meanwhile, *Animal Farm* was an immediate success, radically altering Orwell's finances and dramatically increasing the demand for his work. By 1946 he was publishing regularly in the *Tribune*, the *Manchester Evening News*, the *Observer*, and the *Evening Standard*. In May

ORWELL LIVED AT BARNHILL FARMHOUSE IN SCOTLAND DURING HIS
LAST YEARS OF LIFE.

Orwell moved to Barnhill, a large house remotely located
on the Scottish island of Jura. He was lonely and anxious
to remarry. He proposed to at least two women before
moving to Jura, but neither accepted his offer. After moving to Barnhill, Orwell invited a number of women for
extended visits, hoping that one would decide to stay, but
none did.

That summer Susan Watson followed Orwell to
Barnhill to keep house and care for Richard. When
she arrived, she discovered that Orwell's sister, Avril,
was already there. Avril apparently expected to be housekeeper and nanny for Orwell, and she and Susan did not
get along. After only two months, Susan left Barnhill and
Avril remained.

In August Orwell began work on a new novel, which
was originally titled *The Last Man in Europe*. In October

Orwell visited London, but he did almost no work on the new book while he was there. Throughout 1947 Orwell split his time between his flat in London and the house in Jura. By November he had completed the first draft of the book, which would eventually be called *Nineteen Eighty-Four*.

Orwell was content living on Jura. He enjoyed fishing, hiking, boating, and exploring the island. His work on the new novel was going well, but his long battle with lung problems was beginning to take its toll. Once again he began to cough up blood and was taken to Hairmyres Hospital, where he was diagnosed with tuberculosis. He was treated with streptomycin, a new antibiotic developed in the United States. Although his health improved during the spring, he had a strong reaction to the drug and was warned against returning to the harsher climate of Jura. Nevertheless, he returned to Barnhill where he resumed work on *Nineteen Eighty-Four*. He completed the revision in November 1948, and, unable to find a typist willing to travel to Jura, he typed the manuscript himself.

Orwell's health suffered from the strain of completing *Nineteen Eighty-Four*. In January 1949, just after he finished the novel, he was admitted to Cotswold Sanatorium in Cranham, Gloucestershire. He was still struggling to regain his health in June, when *Nineteen Eighty-Four* was published in Britain and the United States. The book was another immediate success. In his review for the *New Statesman*, V. S. Pritchett wrote that it was "impossible to put the book down." Orville Prescott called *Nineteen Eighty-Four* "a book to haunt your sleep" in his review for the *New York Times*. *Nineteen Eighty-Four* surpassed the high bar set by the success of *Animal Farm* to become Orwell's masterpiece.

Sonia Brownell visited Orwell in the sanatorium, where Orwell proposed marriage. Although she did not love Orwell, she recognized that by marrying him she

ORWELL BEGAN TO COURT SONIA IN 1945, BUT SHE DID NOT BECOME
HIS WIFE UNTIL HE WAS ON HIS DEATHBED FIVE YEARS LATER.

HERE LIES

ERIC ARTHUR BLAIR

BORN JUNE 25TH 1903

DIED JANUARY 21ST 1950

ORWELL'S GRAVESTONE IS IN SUTTON COURTENAY, ENGLAND. IN DEATH, HE IS AGAIN KNOWN AS ERIC ARTHUR BLAIR.

would benefit financially and would be able to manage his literary legacy after he was gone. Her decision was calculated and practical, yet these were the same benefits that Orwell touted in his proposal. After careful consideration, she accepted his offer.

In September he moved to University College Hospital in London. Sonia lived close by and visited him regularly. On October 13 they were married in the hospital. Afterward, she made daily visits to him and began assuming responsibility for his correspondence. She made plans to travel to Switzerland with Orwell on his scheduled release from the hospital on January 25, 1950, but he died of lung failure on January 21, four days before that date arrived.

able, laborious, and short," that "no animal in Engla
ree," and that the "life of an animal is misery and slav
explains that the products of their labor are "stolen
human beings" and that "Man is the only real enemy" o
imals, the cause of their "hunger and overwork." He p
t that "Man is the only creature that consumes without
cing," serving "the interests of no creature except hims
d Major claims that one day there will be a rebellion

(LEFT TO RIGHT) KARL MARX, FRIEDRICH ENGELS, VLADIMIR LENIN,
AND JOSEPH STALIN INSPIRED THE DIRE WORLDS DEPICTED IN ORWELL'S
MOST IMPORTANT WORKS.

ght and day, body and soul, for the overthrow of the h
ce! That is my message to you, comrades: Rebellion!
jor, *Animal Farm*, 30 Old Major points out to the animals
eir "lives are miserable, laborious, and short," that "no
l in England is free," and that the "life of an animal is
y and slavery." He explains that the products of their
e "stolen . . . by human beings" and that "Man is the only
emy" of the animals, the cause of their "hunger and
rk." He points out that "Man is the only creature that

Chapter 2

Orwell and Politics

ORWELL'S WRITING as a novelist, journalist, reviewer, and radio producer cannot be separated from the politics and political philosophies that influenced his work. Nearly everything he wrote was colored by the political energy of the world in which he lived.

Orwell was prosocialism and advocated socialist ideals and opposed all forms of totalitarian government. These attitudes are reflected in his two best-known works: *Animal Farm* and *Nineteen Eighty-Four*, both of which address the dangers of a world in which the working man or woman is oppressed by government for political or economic reasons.

To understand Orwell's dark vision and its continuing relevance to the world in which we live, it is important to understand something of the political movements that shaped his life and his work.

Imperialism and British Colonialism

The term *imperialism* refers to the practice of one nation spreading its influence and control to other nations. It involves the enlargement of an empire beyond traditional borders for the purposes of drawing valuable raw materials, labor, and other economically beneficial items from other regions.

In the nineteenth and early twentieth centuries, Britain was actively involved in expansion. Through the use of force and influence, by 1921 the British government controlled one-quarter of the world's lands and people. Many of the nations that made up the British Empire—nations

such as India, Australia, and Canada—did not become part of Britain. Instead, Britain controlled these nations from a distance and extracted from them whatever the British government deemed valuable for the benefit of Britain. The indigenous people of these countries were often treated as inferior, and the British subjects who were sent there to establish colonies and oversee British interests seldom mingled with them.

Orwell learned from firsthand experience while working in India that imperialism was often cruel and unjust. Scholar William Steinhoff points out that "among the beliefs about life in England which colored . . . [Orwell's] thinking and complicated his opinions about war and patriotism was the idea that the British Empire rested on the labor of millions of exploited 'natives.'"

Orwell said, "When you see how the people live, and still more how easily they die, it is always difficult to believe that you are walking among human beings. All colonial empires are in reality founded upon that fact. . . . Are they really the same flesh as yourself? . . . Or are they merely a kind of undifferentiated brown stuff, about as individual as bees or coral insects? They rise out of the earth, they sweat and starve for a few years, and then they sink back into the nameless mounds of the graveyard and nobody notices that they are gone."

Socialism

The term socialism, like many political terms, has been applied in numerous ways and has been used to refer to quite a few different philosophies and types of political organizations. In Marxist theory socialism referred to an intermediary stage between capitalism and communism. In its most general sense socialism refers to a system of government that works for the benefit of the working class, those who produce labor. Orwell's political views exemplify this distinction between socialism and

communism, as Orwell was highly critical of communism but advocated socialism.

In *Nineteen Eighty-Four* Orwell refers to the philosophy of the totalitarian state of Oceania as Ingsoc, an abbreviation for English socialism. In using this term, Orwell is highlighting how terms are often appropriated and twisted within corrupt governments. The totalitarian government of Oceania opposes the principles for which socialism stands, such as socialism's interest in justice for the working class. The ironic labeling of the political system as English socialism shows how language can be manipulated and misused.

Some, such as economist W. Arthur Lewis, define socialism as a type of democratic society that is classless, thus providing all citizens with an even playing field regardless of their heredity, and preventing groups from establishing themselves as the ruling class. This view is similar to the democratic socialism with which Orwell identified himself.

Communism

Communism, as practiced in the now defunct USSR, was based on the writings of Karl Marx as adapted by Vladimir Lenin for Soviet Russia. Communism advocates the abolition of private property. Under a fully realized communist state, all property—automobiles, real estate, food, farmland, and so on—would be owned by the community.

One of the key differences between socialism and communism, both of which jointly advocate communal ownership of the means of production, is in the distribution of goods. Socialism advocates the equitable sharing of goods among citizens, whereas communism places control over the sharing of goods in the hands of the government. In general, communism transfers more power to the government than socialism. A two-cow analogy is

sometimes used to illustrate this difference. Under socialism, if you have two cows and your neighbor has none, you give your neighbor one of your cows. Under communism, if you have two cows and your neighbor has none, the government takes possession of the cows and distributes the milk. This is an oversimplification of complex political philosophies, which vary greatly in actual practice, but it illustrates the difference in where power is located between the two political systems.

While fighting against fascism in Spain, Orwell was disturbed by the struggles for power he saw among various socialist and communist groups. He felt that they should all be united in a common cause against fascism rather than bickering among themselves.

Fascism

Fascism gets its name from the *Partito Nazionale Fascista*, an Italian group that organized under the leadership of Benito Mussolini to oppose communism during the first part of the twentieth century. Fascism refers to right-wing authoritarian rule; that is, when an individual (in the case of dictators such as Hitler) or a group exercises total control over the population and advocates rigid right-wing ideals, such as the loss of individual freedoms for the benefit of the government. Under fascism the individual citizen is a tool who has no value except in service to the fascist state.

Since the end of World War II, no country directly identifies itself as fascist anymore, as Italy did under Mussolini. Fascism in contemporary history is most associated with Hitler and Germany under his leadership, though Hitler did not refer to himself as a fascist. Some claim that Stalin attributed the term fascist to Hitler to heighten the distinctions between Soviet Russia and Nazi Germany, both of which were totalitarian governments.

Totalitarianism

The term *totalitarianism* is used to refer to any form of government that exercises complete or nearly complete control of every aspect in the lives of its citizens. Any government or state that attempts to coerce all its citizens to support state-sponsored ideology, attempts to control major organizations (such as businesses, political parties, and media), and oppresses those who disagree with the positions mandated by the state has totalitarian leanings. The more aggressively the ruling power exercises its power to suppress those who disagree with its policies and ideas, the more totalitarian it can be said to be; especially when those means of suppression limit individual rights and use unjust practices, such as illegal surveillance and unjust imprisonment, torture, and prosecution to achieve its ends.

In *Animal Farm* Orwell describes a community that moves from communal values toward fascism when the pigs increase their control over the means of production—that is, when they use what the other animals produce for their own benefit. In *Nineteen Eighty-Four* Orwell describes a world that has come under complete totalitarian rule.

, laborious, and short," that "no animal in England is [free]," that the "life of an animal is misery and slavery." [He exp]lains that the products of their labor are "stolen . . . [by hum]an beings" and that "Man is the only real enemy" of th[e animals], the cause of their "hunger and overwork." He points ou[t that Man] is the only creature that consumes without producing," [serving] "the interests of no creature except himself." Old [Major clai]ms that one day there will be a rebellion and animals [will over]throw the tyranny of Man. Work night and day, body and [soul, for] the overthrow of the human race! That is my message t[o you, com]rades: Rebellion! —Old Major, *Animal Farm*, 30 Old Major p[oints out] to the animals that their "lives are miserable, laboriou[s, and shor]t," that "no animal in England is free," and that the "l[ife of an a]nimal is misery and slavery." He explains that the pro[ducts of t]heir labor are "stolen . . . by human beings" and that "M[an is the] only real enemy" of the animals, the cause of their "h[unger and] overwork." He points out that "Man is the only creature [that cons]umes without producing," serving "the interests of no [creature] except himself." Old Major claims that one day there w[ill be a re]bellion and animals will overthrow the tyranny of Man. [Work nigh]t and day, body and soul, for the overthrow of the [human race]! That is my message to you, comrades: Rebellion! —Old [Major, Anim]al *Farm*, 30 Old Major points out to the animals that [their "liv]es are miserable, laborious, and short," that "no anim[al in Eng]land is free," and that the "life of an animal is miser[y and slav]ery." He explains that the products of their labor are "s[tolen . . .] by human beings" and that "Man is the only real ene[my" of the] animals, the cause of their "hunger and overwork." He [points out] that "Man is the only creature that consumes without p[roducing,]" serving "the interests of no creature except himself.[Old Majo]r claims that one day there will be a rebellion and an[imals will] overthrow the tyranny of Man. Work night and day, bod[y and soul], for the overthrow of the human race! That is my messa[ge to you,] comrades: Rebellion! —Old Major, *Animal Farm*, 30 Old [Major poin]ts out to the animals that their "lives are miserable, [laboriou]s, and short," that "no animal in England is free," and [that the]"life of an animal is misery and slavery." He explains [that the]products of their labor are "stolen . . . by human beings[" and that] "Man is the only real enemy" of the animals, the cau[se of thei]r "hunger and overwork." He points out that "Man is the [only crea]ture that consumes without producing," serving "the i[nterests] of no creature except himself." Old Major claims that on[e day]

Part II:
The Writing of
George Orwell

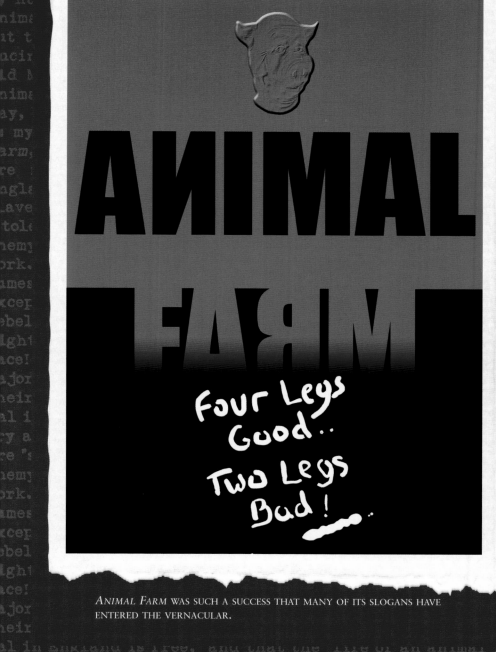

ANIMAL FARM

Four Legs Good.. Two Legs Bad !

ANIMAL FARM WAS SUCH A SUCCESS THAT MANY OF ITS SLOGANS HAVE
ENTERED THE VERNACULAR.

Chapter 1

George Orwell's *Animal Farm*

Overview of *Animal Farm*

Perhaps the most important fact to keep in mind when reading *Animal Farm* is that it is an allegorical satire—a work that is both satire and allegory. Satire is a literary genre that uses wit and humor to criticize something, such as human behaviors, forms of government, ideas, religions, and so on. In *Animal Farm* Orwell satirizes Russian communism. Scholar Northrup Frye notes that "*Animal Farm* adopts one of the classical formulas of satire, the corruption of principle by expediency." *Animal Farm* begins with a set of principles that would improve the lives of the animals, but human nature (or "pig" nature) corrupts these principles for the purposes of immediate gain.

A work is an allegory when the characters and/or events represent people, ideas, and events beyond the narrative. In *Animal Farm* some of the characters represent people. For example, Napoleon represents Soviet dictator Joseph Stalin; Snowball represents Soviet politician Leon Trotsky; Mr. Jones represents Czar Nicholas II of Russia; and so on. Some of the characters represent groups: the hard-working Boxer represents the working class and Napoleon's dogs represent the Soviet secret police. Other characters represent things, such as the smooth-talking Squealer, who stands for the Soviet propaganda newspaper *Pravda*. Objects also function as allegories. The ribbons and sugar that Mollie craves symbolize luxuries available under the former czar. Sugarcandy Mountain symbolizes the Christian ideal of heaven.

The events that take place parallel actual historical events. The first rebellion of the animals represents the

55

Russian Revolution of 1917. Snowball leading the animals in the battle of Cowshed represents Trotsky's mobilization of the Red Army in the Soviet Civil War (1918–1919). The novel ends with a parallel to the Tehran Conference of 1943, a meeting attended by Joseph Stalin, U.S. President Franklin Roosevelt, and British Prime Minister Winston Churchill, during which the three leaders devised plans to defeat Nazi Germany.

The Principal Characters in *Animal Farm*

The Main Animals

Napoleon (pig)
Napoleon is a Berkshire boar. Orwell describes him early in the novel as a quiet, "fierce-looking" young pig (35).
Based on Soviet dictator Joseph Stalin, who ruled Russia until his death in 1953.

Snowball (pig)
Snowball, like Napoleon, is one of two boars that the farmer, Mr. Jones, is "breeding for sale" (35). He is "more vivacious . . . quicker in speech and more inventive" than Napoleon, but does not have the same "depth of character" (35).
Based on Leon Trotsky, head of the Russian Red Army during the revolution and influential political figure in the early days of Soviet Russia. Trotsky came to oppose Stalin and was exiled from Russia and then assassinated.

Boxer (cart horse)
Boxer is the most loyal and most productive worker on Animal Farm. His two maxims are: "Napoleon is always

right" and "I will work harder," thus emphasizing loyalty to the leader and productivity.

Suggests working-class figures such as Alexey Stakhanov, a Russian miner who was touted as an example of the greatness of the worker in Soviet Russia.

Old Major (boar)

Old Major, "the prize Middle White boar" on the farm (25), is twelve years old and "majestic-looking" (26). His ideas spur the rebellion.

Based on Karl Marx and Vladimir Lenin.

Mollie (horse)

Mollie is a white mare who pulled Mr. Jones's carriage prior to the revolution. She is marked by her vanity.

Suggests anticommunist Russians, known as White Russians, who opposed the revolution and fought against the Red Army.

Moses (raven)

Moses is a tame raven that Mr. Jones keeps as a pet. He is a "clever talker" who spies for Mr. Jones and tells the other animals stories of "a mysterious country called Sugarcandy Mountain" where animals supposedly go when they die (37).

Suggests the Roman Catholic and Russian Orthodox churches.

Squealer (pig)

Like all the other pigs on the farm, except Napoleon and Snowball (the two boars), Squealer is a porker. He is a "brilliant" and "persuasive" talker (36).

Suggests Pravda and other sources of Soviet propaganda.

Dogs
The nine dogs are trained in secret by Napoleon to be vicious and obedient. Their brutality makes Napoleon's rise to power possible.
Suggests the Soviet secret police.

Minimus (pig)
Minimus has a talent for composing songs and poems.
Suggests communist poet Vladimir Mayakovsky, who was the premier poet of the Russian Revolution.

Other Animals

Muriel (white goat)
Muriel reads better than many of the other animals and is often called upon to read the commandments to those, such as the horses, who are not literate enough.

Clover (cart horse)
Clover is "a stout motherly mare" (26) who is sensitive to the injustices suffered by the animals as Napoleon's rule spins out of control.

Benjamin (donkey)
Benjamin is the "oldest animal on the farm" and the "worst tempered" (26). His comments are often cynical and he frequently refuses to involve himself in the many debates and conversations that take place on the farm.

Jessie, Bluebell, and Pincher (dogs)
Their offspring are trained by Napoleon to support his ambitions with violence.

The Cat
The laziest of the animals. The cat disappears whenever

there is "work to be done," and reappears "at meal-times" (47).

The People

Mr. Jones
Mr. Jones owns Manor Farm. The name Manor Farm brings to mind the manor house, an upper-class home in which people of privilege and wealth (families who own land) live. In making Mr. Jones a disagreeable alcoholic, Orwell is commenting on the moral decay of the upper classes—those who profit from the suffering of the working class (the animals in the novel).
Based on Russian Czar Nicholas II.

Mr. Pilkington of Foxwood Farm
Mr. Pilkington is "an easy going gentleman farmer who . . . [spends] most of his time in fishing or hunting" (54–55). His farm, Foxwood, is "a large, neglected, old-fashioned farm, much overgrown by woodland, with all its pastures worn out and its hedges in a disgraceful condition" (54).
Suggests Winston Churchill and England.

Mr. Frederick of Pinchfield Farm
Mr. Frederick is "a tough, shrewd man, perpetually involved in lawsuits and with a name for driving hard bargains" (55). His farm, Pinchfield, is "smaller and better kept" (55) than Foxwood.
Suggests Hitler and Germany. The name is based on Frederick II, who was King of Prussia from 1740–1786 and a role model for Hitler.

Mr. Whymper
Mr. Whymper is a solicitor who acts as an intermediary for Napoleon's business dealings with humans. Whymper

is described as a "sly-looking little man with side whiskers, a solicitor in a very small way of business" (77). *Suggests Western journalists and business interests.*

Summary

Chapter I

Animal Farm begins one night after Mr. Jones, the owner of Manor Farm, falls asleep after a night of drinking. Old Major, an award-winning boar and the most respected animal on the farm, has called a meeting that all the animals attend, except Moses, Mr. Jones's tame raven. Old Major has grown old and realizes that he will soon die. He has called the animals together to tell them of a dream he had the night before and to "pass on" his wisdom about "the nature of life on this earth" (28).

Old Major is the voice of Karl Marx and Vladimir Lenin, whose philosophies underscored the communist revolution in Russia. Like Marx and Lenin, Old Major's concerns are for the workers, the animals that produce the goods for the farm but do not reap the benefits.

Old Major points out to the animals that their "lives are miserable, laborious, and short," that "no animal in England is free," and that the "life of an animal is misery and slavery" (28). He explains that the products of their labor are "stolen . . . by human beings" (28) and that "Man is the only real enemy" of the animals, the cause of their "hunger and overwork." He points out that "Man is the only creature that consumes without producing" (29), serving "the interests of no creature except himself" (30–31). Old Major claims that one day there will be a rebellion and animals will overthrow the tyranny of Man.

> Work night and day, body and soul, for the overthrow of the human race! That is my message to

you, comrades: Rebellion!
—Old Major, *Animal Farm*, 30

When four rats creep into the meeting, creating an uproar among the animals, Old Major tells them that "wild creatures, such as rats and rabbits" (which represent peasants in Orwell's allegory) are their friends. After the animals vote in agreement that the wild animals are their friends, Old Major lays out some of the basic principles that will guide the animals—"Whatever goes upon two legs is an enemy. Whatever goes upon four legs, or has wings, is a friend"—and cautions them to "remember . . . that in fighting against Man . . . [they] must not come to resemble him" (31). This foreshadows the conclusion in Chapter X when the pigs are said to resemble people.

Old Major sets down some guidelines to avoid becoming like Man, which animals should do because "all habits of Man are evil":

1. No animal must ever live in a house,
2. or sleep in a bed,
3. or wear clothes,
4. or drink alcohol,
5. or smoke tobacco,
6. or touch money,
7. or engage in trade . . .
8. no animal must ever tyrannise over his own kind . . .
9. [and] no animal must ever kill any other animal.

Animal Farm, 31–32

Finally, Old Major describes his dream, in which he saw a world free of Man's influence. He teaches the animals a song called "Beasts of England," which he learned in his youth. The song is comprised of seven stanzas and speaks

of "the golden future time" when animals are free from the tyranny of man. One stanza reads:

> Soon or late the day is coming,
> Tyrant Man shall be o'erthrown,
> And the fruitful fields of England
> Shall be trod by beasts alone.

The animals sing the song with fervor, awakening Mr. Jones who, thinking a fox has entered the farm, fires his gun into the yard, sending all the animals racing to their beds.

Historical Parallels in Chapter I

Old Major is the voice of Marxist-Leninism. Karl Marx (1818–1883) was a philosopher and revolutionary who wrote The Communist Manifesto *in 1848, a book that provided the early philosophical basis for communism. The work is about the dynamic relationship between oppressors and those they oppress. Vladimir Lenin (1870–1924), a Russian revolutionary, adopted and extended the theories of Marx and argued that capitalism and imperialism can only be overthrown by revolution. Lenin led the October Revolution in 1917, which overthrew the existing Russian government and installed the Bolsheviks, or Communists. The song "Beasts of England" represents "L'Internationale," a French song that was the anthem for communist, socialist, and anarchist movements during the twentieth century.*

Chapter II

Chapter II begins three days after the meeting in the barn. Old Major has died in his sleep and the pigs, who are among the more intelligent animals on the farm,

have begun to prepare for the Rebellion, with the two boars, Napoleon and Snowball, assuming leadership roles. Napoleon, Snowball, and Squealer develop a "system of thought" (36), establishing the theoretical groundwork for the Rebellion, which they call Animalism.

The animals hold secret meetings at night, during which the pigs help the other animals to understand the rebellion. The "stupidest questions" (36) are asked by Mollie, the white mare, who wants to know if she will still be allowed to wear ribbons in her mane and eat sugar after the Rebellion. Mollie, whose vanity has been massaged by special gifts from Mr. Jones, is reluctant to embrace the Rebellion, just as some Russians who benefited from oppression were reluctant to support the Russian Revolution.

Also at odds with the idea of Rebellion is Moses, the raven, who tells the animals about Sugarcandy Mountain (i.e., Heaven), a paradise where they will all go when they die. Moses's stories of Sugarcandy Mountain represent how religion was used to keep people from resisting the existing economic, social, and political structure in Russia prior to the Revolution. To paraphrase what Marx wrote in *the Critique of Hegel's Philosophy of Right* in 1843, "Religion . . . is the opium of the people."

In June the men who work for Mr. Jones forget to feed the animals and go hunting, while Mr. Jones gets drunk and passes out in the drawing room. The hungry animals break into the store-shed to find something to eat. The next day Jones and his men come with whips to punish the animals. They fight back, and the men are driven from the farm.

> They woke at dawn as usual, and suddenly remembering the glorious thing that had happened, they all raced out into the pasture together.

> . . . Yes, it was theirs—everything that they could see was theirs! In the ecstasy of that thought they gamboled round and round, they hurled themselves into the air in great leaps of excitement.
> *Animal Farm*, 40

The Rebellion had occurred, and the animals had won with ease. They immediately set about to get rid of all the objects of oppression around the farm. They throw knives, bits, dog chains, and nose rings down the well. They burn halters, blinkers, nosebags, and whips. After celebrating and singing "Beasts of England," which had become their anthem, they go to bed.

The next day they awake as free animals. Snowball and Napoleon, the leaders of the animals, break into the farmhouse. They remove hams they find hanging in the kitchen and bury them. Boxer kicks in a barrel of beer they find in the kitchen. They decide that the farmhouse should remain as a museum, but that no animals should live there.

The name of Manor Farm is changed to Animal Farm and the theory of Animalism is reduced to seven commandments that the animals are to follow. Snowball paints them on the wall of the barn where all the animals can see them:

1. Whatever goes upon two legs is an enemy.
2. Whatever goes upon four legs, or has wings, is a friend.
3. No animal shall wear clothes.
4. No animal shall sleep in a bed.
5. No animal shall drink alcohol.
6. No animal shall kill any other animal.
7. All animals are equal.

Afterward, following Snowball's lead, the animals set off to bring in the hay harvest, after first milking the cows. When the animals want to know what will become of all the milk, Napoleon stands in front of the buckets and tells the animals that they should not concern themselves with the milk. When the animals return at the end of the day, the milk is missing, the first clue that the rebellion may not lead to the ends Old Major had imagined.

Historical Parallels in Chapter II

The Rebellion represents the October Revolution (1917), which installed a communist regime in the Soviet Union. Jones represents Czar Nicholas II of Russia, who was removed from power by the revolution. The two boars, Snowball and Napoleon, represent the two key figures in the revolution: Trotsky and Stalin. The raven, Moses, represents the Roman Catholic and Russian Orthodox churches.

Animalism is Animal Farm's version of dialectical materialism, the philosophical position based on Marx's social history, which maintains that history is the history of class struggles and that forces in those class struggles are at odds with one another. Mollie's questions represent the attitudes of the "white Russians," a group of anti-Bolsheviks (Bolsheviks were a part of the Marxist Russian Social Democratic Labour Party, which became the Communist Party of the Soviet Union after the revolution).

Chapter III

In this chapter Orwell portrays the much improved living conditions on the farm. The animals work diligently to bring in the hay harvest. The cleverest of the group, the pigs, assume supervisory roles, directing the labor of the others, while Boxer distinguishes himself as a loyal

and dedicated worker. The animals do not steal, fight, or complain, and nearly everyone contributes to the welfare of the farm. The two exceptions are Mollie, who had been favored under the oppression of Mr. Jones and who tends to get up late and leave work early, and the cat, who disappears "when there [is] work to be done" (47).

> Everyone worked according to his capacity. . . . Nobody stole, nobody grumbled of his rations, the quarreling and biting and jealousy which had been normal features of life in the old days had almost disappeared.
> *Animal Farm*, 47

The animals do not work on Sundays. Instead, they assemble in the barn where they discuss issues and put forth resolutions on which the animals vote. A flag is made from one of Mrs. Jones's green tablecloths. A white hoof and horn are painted on the flag. The flag stands for "the future Republic of Animals"(48). Differences between Snowball and Napoleon are further accentuated. The two boars are the most vocal and active and, along with the pigs, put forth most of the resolutions, as many of the other animals are not clever enough to think of any. But Snowball and Napoleon, we learn, are seldom in agreement.

Snowball organizes the other animals into "Animal Committees," such as the "Egg Production Committee" and the "Clean Tails League." A system is set up to educate all the animals and to make them as literate as possible. The pigs and the dogs excel in reading and writing, though the dogs prefer only to read the seven commandments painted on the barn. Boxer only manages to learn the first four letters of the alphabet. To help the less literate animals, Snowball reduces the seven commandments to one maxim: "Four legs good, two legs bad" (50), which

is painted on the wall above the seven commandments, and which the sheep begin to bleat frequently.

Napoleon takes no interest in the committees and concerns himself with "the education of the young," which he argues is most important. When Jessie and Bluebell give birth to nine puppies, Napoleon takes them away after they are weaned, claiming that he will be "responsible for their education" (51). He secludes them from the other animals and they are forgotten.

Chapter III ends with the animals discovering that the missing milk is being added to the pigs' mash and that the early apples that fall from the trees are to be gathered for the pigs, rather than shared equally. Squealer convinces the other animals that this is necessary because the pigs, as the "brainworkers," need the additional nutrition (52).

Historical Parallels in Chapter III

The hoof and horn on the flag the animals create is Animal Farm's version of the hammer and sickle, symbols representing communism that are found on the red Soviet flag. The disagreement between Snowball and Napoleon parallel disagreements between Trotsky and Stalin after the revolution.

Chapter IV

By Chapter IV news of the rebellion on Animal Farm has spread. Snowball and Napoleon send pigeons to tell animals at other farms of their success, and Mr. Jones, who spends most of his time drinking at a bar in Willingdon, spreads news of the loss of his farm. Other farmers consider ways to work Mr. Jones's misfortune to their advantage.

Two of the farmers that learn of the rebellion are Mr. Pilkingkton, who owns Foxwood Farm, and Mr.

Frederick, who owns Pinchfield. Pilkington and Frederick are troubled by the rebellion, fearing that their own animals might get wind of it and take similar action on their farms. They spread rumors that the animals running Animal Farm are starving, fighting among themselves, torturing each other, and practicing cannibalism. Despite this, the song "Beasts of England" spreads, even though animals are whipped for singing it.

Jones, the men who worked for him, and five other volunteers attempt to take Animal Farm back from the animals. Armed mostly with sticks, they attack, but the animals are prepared, successfully repelling the assault. During the fight, Boxer kills one of the men and Snowball, who distinguishes himself in battle, is wounded when Jones's bullet grazes his back.

> "He is dead," said Boxer sorrowfully. "I had no intention of doing that. I forgot that I was wearing iron shoes. Who will believe that I did not do this on purpose?"
>
> "No sentimentality, comrade!" cried Snowball, from whose wounds the blood was still dripping. "War is war. The only good human being is a dead one."
>
> "I have no wish to take life, not even human life," repeated Boxer, and his eyes were full of tears.
> *Animal Farm*, 58–59

The animals rejoice at their victory, sing "Beasts of England," and award Snowball and Boxer with medals signifying "Animal Hero, First Class." The battle is christened "The Battle of the Cowshed," and October 12, the day of the battle, becomes a day of celebration, joining "Midsummer Day," which marks the day of the Rebellion.

Historical Parallels in Chapter IV

The reactions of Pilkington of Foxwood Farm and Frederick of Pinchfield Farm represent the reactions of Churchill and England and Hitler and Germany to the rise of communism in Russia. The Battle of the Cowshed stands for the Russian Civil War, which ended with the establishment of the Soviet Union in 1922. Snowball's leadership in battle parallels Trotsky's leadership of the Red Army.

Chapter V

In Chapter V the story moves into winter. Mollie, who did not fight in the Battle of the Cowshed, and who had been

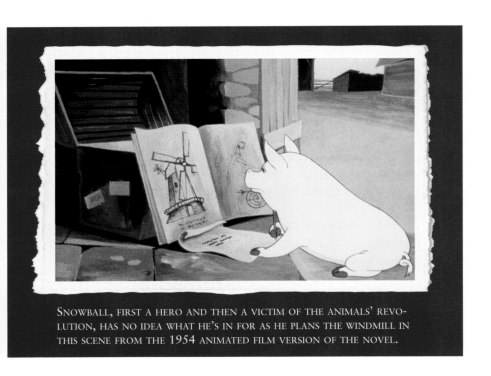

SNOWBALL, FIRST A HERO AND THEN A VICTIM OF THE ANIMALS' REVOLUTION, HAS NO IDEA WHAT HE'S IN FOR AS HE PLANS THE WINDMILL IN THIS SCENE FROM THE 1954 ANIMATED FILM VERSION OF THE NOVEL.

caught by Clover talking to one of Mr. Pilkington's men across the hedge separating the two farms, disappears. Word reaches the farm that Mollie is pulling a dogcart for a man who owns a bar. Mollie symbolizes those who preferred the oppression of Czarist Russia to the relative freedom of Soviet rule.

The cold weather makes work impossible, so the animals spend their time planning for the next season. Snowball and Napoleon continue to be at odds with one another. Snowball offers numerous suggestions for the farm, while Napoleon, who offers no suggestions, opposes Snowball's ideas, the most significant of which is his plan to build a windmill. This would provide electricity for the farm and make all their lives easier. Napoleon vigorously opposes the building of the windmill, but after great debate, the animals side with Snowball. Napoleon is unwilling to concede and produces a whining sound that summons the nine dogs he has been "educating" in secret. They are now large and ferocious and violently chase Snowball forever from the farm.

> Napoleon produced no schemes of his own, but said quietly that Snowball's would come to nothing, and seemed to be biding his time. But of all their controversies, none was so bitter as the one that took place over the windmill.
> *Animal Farm*, 63

His authority now forcibly established, Napoleon announces to the terrified animals that there will be no more Sunday meetings. All decisions will now be made by "a special committee of pigs, presided over by himself" (68). The animals will gather on Sundays only to sing "Beasts of England" and receive their orders.

Squealer begins a propaganda campaign to convince the animals that Napoleon is a great leader making sacrifices on their behalf and that Snowball is a criminal. He

explains away Snowball's bravery at the Battle of the Cowshed, claiming that "Bravery is not enough. . . . Loyalty and obedience are more important," and that Snowball's bravery was "much exaggerated" (70). Squealer is convincing, and the animals adopt the general opinion voiced by Boxer, who says, "If Comrade Napoleon says it, it must be right" (70).

At the next Sunday meeting, Napoleon, Squealer, and a pig named Minimus sit on a high platform above the other animals, the nine dogs in a semicircle in front of them and the other pigs behind. Three weeks after Napoleon seized power by driving Snowball from the farm, Napoleon announces that the animals will be building the windmill. At first the animals are shocked, but Squealer tells them that Napoleon had never opposed the windmill and that Snowball had actually stolen the plans from Napoleon. With the help of three growling dogs and a clever tongue, Squealer is able to convince the animals that what he is telling them is true.

Historical Parallels in Chapter V

Like Snowball and Napoleon, Trotsky and Stalin argued for different focuses after the revolution. Trotsky called for an increased focus on industry, as Snowball calls for the building of the windmill, and Stalin called for an increased focus on agriculture, as Napoleon emphasizes education of the young. Squealer is the personification of propaganda—the manipulation of information to support a particular cause (with little concern over the accuracy of the information). The leading vehicle for propaganda in Russia was the newspaper, Pravda.

At the start of the Russian Revolution, a secret police force was established. This force evolved into an organization that implemented a campaign of terror against anyone who might oppose communism. In Animal Farm, *the function of the secret police is fulfilled by Napoleon's*

dogs. The dogs drive Snowball from the farm just as Stalin drove Trotsky into exile in Almaty, Kazakhstan (then called Alma-Ata), in 1928. Stalin increasingly bent the truth to make his position more appealing to the people, spreading lies about Trotsky and others who opposed him. In Chapter IV we see Napoleon beginning to control information in the same way by claiming that he, not Snowball, was the original designer of the windmill.

Minimus represents the Russian poet, Vladimir Mayakovsky, a prosocialist who labeled his work "communist futurism" and produced left-wing poems and proworker posters.

Chapter VI

Chapter VI covers the next year, during which time the animals work "like slaves" (73) sixty hours per week. Napoleon implements half days of work on Sunday, which is supposed to be voluntary, but animals who do not work have their food rations reduced by 50 percent. The animals work hard, but the crop is less successful than the previous year, despite the increased hours. Boxer works the hardest. Each time the farm seems to be struggling, he proclaims, "I will work harder," and increases his efforts.

Napoleon announces in the summer that he will begin trading with neighboring farms, claiming that trade is necessary to provide the animals with materials they cannot produce on the farm, such as nails and iron for horses' shoes. He arranges to sell hay, part of the wheat crop, and eggs.

The animals grow uneasy, as they do each time the running of the farm takes a shift away from Old Major's original vision, but they are either swayed by propaganda or silenced by the growling dogs. Napoleon's intermediary between Animal Farm and the outside world is a solicitor from Willingdon named Mr. Whymper.

When animals recall rules against using money, Squealer convinces them that such rules never existed, that they were lies circulated by Snowball.

> Once again the animals were conscious of a vague uneasiness. Never to have any dealings with human beings, never to engage in trade, never to make use of money—had not these been among the earliest resolutions passed at that first triumphant Meeting after Jones was expelled?
> *Animal Farm*, 76

Meanwhile, the pigs move into the farmhouse, claiming that, as the "brains of the farm," the quiet of the farmhouse was necessary and "more suited to the dignity of the Leader" (79), which was what they had come to call Napoleon.

Boxer responds to the changes by claiming, as always, that "Napoleon is always right" (70), but Clover has reservations. She asks Muriel to read her the Fourth Commandment on the barn wall. The commandment now reads, "No animal shall sleep in a bed *with sheets*" (79). Clover, like most of the animals, cannot remember precisely how the commandments were phrased, but doesn't recall any mention of sheets. Squealer, once again, is able to convince her that there was never a prohibition against beds.

The pigs now sleep an additional hour in the morning.

Because of the sale of some of the harvest, the animals have less food. With approaching winter, fierce southwest winds rise up and destroy all the work that has been done on the windmill. The animals, who have worked hard on the windmill while also tending the rest of the farm, are devastated. Napoleon sniffs about the ruins and declares that the windmill was not destroyed by the storm, but by Snowball. He claims that Snowball probably came from neighboring Foxwood Farm. The animals are shocked and cry out against Snowball.

At the close of the chapter, Napoleon announces that the animals will work through the winter, "rain or shine," to rebuild the windmill (82–83).

Historical Parallels in Chapter VI

The destruction of the windmill in Chapter VI represents the failure of Stalin's first Five-Year Plan to strengthen Russia's economy, which resulted in hunger and severe decreases in grain production. Mr. Whymper, with whom Napoleon begins a relationship, stands for Western journalists who helped relay Stalin's messages to the rest of the world, and the deals Napoleon negotiates with Whymper suggests the Treaty of Rapallo, an agreement signed between Russia and Germany in 1922. Napoleon's blaming of Snowball for the destruction of the windmill parallels Stalin's blaming of Trotsky for hardships experienced under his rule.

Chapter VII

Winter is harsh, and life becomes increasingly difficult for the animals. Food shortages lead to reduced rations and rumors of hardships on the farm continue to spread among local humans. Napoleon uses tricks to convince Mr. Whymper that the farm is still doing well, but his demands on the animals increase.

Napoleon rarely appears around the farm anymore, and when he does venture out he is guarded by the dogs. He sends Squealer to tell the hens that they will have to give up their eggs so that he can fulfill a contract he has signed. When three hens rebel, he cuts off their food rations and announces that anyone who gives the hens food will be put to death. In the end the hens give in, but only after nine of them have died.

One of Napoleon's business deals involved the sale of some lumber, which both Mr. Pilkington and Mr. Frederick wanted. Napoleon's negotiations flip-flopped

between the two. Each time he favored one farmer, he would claim that Snowball was hiding in the other farm. So if negotiations were going well with Foxwood Farm, word would circulate that Snowball was hiding at Pinchfield, and vice versa.

By spring anything that went wrong on the farm was attributed to mischief caused by Snowball, though no one had seen Snowball since he was driven away. The animals are told that Snowball was in league with Mr. Jones the entire time and that, contrary to what the animals believed, Snowball was working against them at the Battle of the Cowshed. Squealer manages to convince the animals that, rather than fighting bravely as the animals remember, Snowball had fled the fight and Napoleon was the one who had saved them. He further claims that Snowball has spies among the animals.

A few days later, Napoleon assembles the animals in the yard and appears wearing two medals: "Animal Hero, First Class" and "Animal Hero, Second Class." His dogs drag four pigs—the four who had protested when Napoleon ended Sunday meetings—in front of him, where they are made to confess their "crimes" and that they had been in contact with Snowball. They are then executed. Next come the three hens who had resisted Napoleon's attempt to take their eggs. They are made to confess and then killed. Other animals are forced to confess to working with Snowball and then slaughtered. When it was all over, the remaining animals are shocked that so many had been working secretly for Snowball.

The tale of confessions and executions went on, until there was a pile of corpses lying before Napoleon's feet and the air was heavy with the smell of blood.
Animal Farm, 93

Clover realizes, more than the other animals, that things on the farm have gone in a strange direction:

> As Clover looked down the hillside her eyes filled with tears. If she could have spoken her thoughts, it would have been to say that. . . . these scenes of terror and slaughter were not what they had looked forward to on that night when Old Major first stirred them to rebellion. . . . They had come to a time when no one dared speak his mind, when fierce, growling dogs roamed everywhere, and when you had to watch your comrades torn to pieces after confessing to shocking crimes.
> *Animal Farm, 95*

Nevertheless, Clover remains faithful, even after Squealer announces that "Beasts of England" has been banned and that the animals are no longer permitted to sing it. The song is replaced by one composed by the pig, Minimus, which begins:

> "Animal Farm, Animal Farm,
> Never through me shalt thou come to harm!"
> *Animal Farm, 97*

This section of the novel represents a significant shift away from loyalty to the ideas of Old Major or the animals toward loyalty to the state.

Historical Parallels in Chapter VII

When Napoleon reaches an agreement with Frederick, Orwell is alluding to the pact signed between the Soviet Union and Hitler's Germany in 1939 in which the two countries reached an agreement about which countries and areas each would avoid. This agreement allowed

Hitler to continue his fascist expansion into Europe with-
out threat of Russian intervention.

In the 1930s Stalinist Russia began a campaign to
purge the Communist Party of saboteurs. A group called
the Commissariat of Internal Affairs (NKVD), run by a
former member of the secret police, would force members
to confess to treason and then execute them. Known as
The Great Purge and The Great Terror, the group's activ-
ities were brutal. In some cases the children of supposed
traitors were executed. The slaughter of the animals in
Animal Farm *reenacts this brutality.*

Chapter VIII

Several days after Napoleon's executions, the animals
check the commandments on the barn wall and discover
that the sixth commandment now mysteriously reads:
"No animal shall kill any other animal *without cause*"
(98). Again, the animals do not remember the final words
being there, but the wall is proof enough for them.

All successes on the farm are now attributed to him.
The hens, for example, now say, "Under the guidance of
our Leader, Comrade Napoleon, I have laid five eggs in six
days" (100). Minimus composes a poem praising
Napoleon, which Squealer paints on the wall of the barn
opposite the seven commandments.

Negotiations for the lumber continue with Mr.
Frederick and Mr. Pilkington. When one or the other
makes an unacceptable offer, rumors spread around the
farm that the men of that farm are plotting an attack
on Animal Farm and that Snowball has been seen on
the farm. The animals are now told that Snowball
never received the honor of "Animal Hero, First
Class," and had instead been "censured for showing
cowardice" (103).

Despite the hardship now confronting the animals on the farm, the windmill is finished. Napoleon names it Napoleon Mill. Two days later Napoleon announces that he has sold the timber to Frederick and that the animals should replace the phrase "death to Frederick" with "death to Pinchfield" (104). A few days later, when it is discovered that the bank notes paid by Frederick are forgeries, Napoleon, in a rage, pronounces a death sentence on Frederick. He sends pigeons to Pilkington to attempt reconciliation, but it is too late. When Frederick and his men attack the farm, Pilkington's response is, "Serves you right" (107).

> Frederick and his men had halted about the windmill. The animals watched them, and a murmur of dismay went round. Two of the men had produced a crowbar and a sledge hammer. They were going to knock the windmill down.
> *Animal Farm*, 107

With great effort and many casualties, the animals manage to keep the men from overrunning the farm, but not before Frederick's men blow up the newly completed windmill, leaving behind nothing to show for the animals' two years of hard work. The animals are shaken by the attack and their losses, but Napoleon and the pigs declare a great victory and Napoleon creates the Order of the Green Banner, which he awards to himself.

A few days later, the animals hear a ruckus in the farmhouse. The pigs, who found a barrel of whiskey, have gotten drunk. They sing a drunken version of "Beasts of England," and Napoleon is seen wearing Mr. Jones's bowler hat. Napoleon, who is unaccustomed to alcohol, becomes sick. Squealer announces that Napoleon is dying, but the next day Napoleon recovers and makes the drinking of alcohol punishable by death. Despite this decree, a

week later Napoleon announces that a small paddock, which was to be used for animals in retirement, would be used instead to grow barley.

The chapter ends when the animals hear a large crash in the barn and discover Squealer lying next to a broken ladder. The dogs escort him back to the farmhouse and the animals now notice that they have misremembered yet another commandment. The Fifth Commandment now reads: "No animal shall drink alcohol *to excess*" (113).

Historical Parallels in Chapter VIII

In 1941, Germany broke its nonaggression pact with the Soviet Union and invaded Russia. Animal Farm's version of this event is Frederick's betrayal of the timber sale and the resulting attack by Frederick's men on the farm. The Order of the Green Banner is fashioned after the Order of the Red Banner, which began as a decoration given to heroes of the revolution, and the Order of Lenin, which supplanted the Order of the Red Banner as the Soviet Union's highest decoration.

Chapter IX

Chapter IX opens with Boxer, who is recovering from the wounds he received during the battle with Frederick's men, thinking of his eventual retirement. Boxer is eleven and, according to the original setup of Animal Farm, will retire when he is twelve. Then he will be able to spend the rest of his life relaxing after all his hard work.

The winter is hard and, once again, rations for all animals except the pigs and dogs are reduced. New litters of pigs are born, all sired by Napoleon, and they are instructed to avoid playing with the other animals. Other animals are told to stand aside when a pig passes, and pigs begin wearing green ribbons on their tails on Sundays.

Workloads for the other animals are increased and the pigs begin making alcohol in Jones's brew-house with the barley from the converted field. Each pig receives a pint of beer daily. Napoleon receives a gallon.

In April it is announced that the farm has become a republic. An election for president is held, with Napoleon as the only candidate. The story of the Battle of the Cowshed is changed again. This time Snowball is said to have been leading the humans and calling out "Long Live Humanity!" (119). The animals are told that Snowball's wound was a result of a bite from Napoleon. Moses, the raven, returns to the farm with stories of Sugarcandy Mountain and how animals can look forward to better days after they have died. The pigs claim that Moses's tales are lies, but allow him to spread stories freely among the other animals.

Boxer continues to work hard to make a good start on rebuilding the windmill before he retires, but one day he falls. His lung has given out. Boxer is confident that the other animals can now complete the windmill without him and is hoping to be put out to pasture. Napoleon sends word that he has arranged for Boxer to be sent to a hospital for treatment, but two days later when a van arrives to take Boxer away, Benjamin notices that written on the side of the van is "Alfred Simmonds, Horse Slaughterer and Glue Boiler, Willingdon. Dealer in Hides and Bone-Meal. Kennels Supplied" (123). The animals are horrified and try to stop the van, but they are too late. Three days later they learn that Boxer died in the "hospital." Squealer claims to have been at Boxer's bedside when he died and said that the rumor about Boxer being sent to a glue factory is wicked and false. The van, he claimed, had merely been converted and the hospital had not yet had time to paint out the old name.

The next Sunday Napoleon makes a rare appearance to praise Boxer and remind the animals of Boxer's two favorite maxims: "I will work hard" and "Comrade

Napoleon is always right" (126). The pigs plan a banquet in Boxer's honor. A grocery van arrives one day and the animals hear a noisy celebration in the farmhouse. The next day word circulates that the pigs have found money for another case of whiskey.

> Too late, someone thought of racing ahead and shutting the five-barred gate; but in another moment the van was through it and rapidly disappearing down the road. Boxer was never seen again.
> *Animal Farm*, 124

Napoleon's betrayal of Boxer, the farm's most loyal worker, epitomizes the ultimate betrayal of all the animals by the pigs.

Historical Parallels in Chapter IX

Boxer's qualities parallel those ascribed to Soviet miner Alexey Stakhanov, who became an example of loyalty and productivity in Soviet Russia. Though many of Stakhanov's accomplishments turned out to be propaganda created by the Soviet government to induce more productivity from workers, at the time Orwell was writing Animal Farm, *Stakhanov was seen as an ideal worker, in one instance producing fourteen times his quota of coal. The unjust selling of Boxer to the slaughterer symbolizes the Communist Party's betrayal of the workers.*

Chapter X

Chapter X projects us years into the future after many of the animals have died and few animals remember the early days of the rebellion. Napoleon and Squealer have grown fat. Animal Farm is prosperous, but life for the animals is difficult. They work hard and believe what they are told

about Animalism. The windmill is complete, but is used for milling corn for profit rather than providing comfort and relief to the animals. Napoleon says that the "truest happiness . . . lies in working hard and living frugally" (128).

> There was a deadly silence. Amazed, terrified, huddling together, the animals watched the long line of pigs march slowly round the yard. It was as though the world had turned upside-down.
> *Animal Farm*, 132

Only the pigs and dogs benefit from the prosperity of the farm. The other animals—the workers—are often hungry and cold. Benjamin came to believe that "hunger, hardship, and disappointment . . . [were] the unalterable

BURY FARM, IN WALLINGTON, ENGLAND, WAS THOUGHT TO BE THE FARM ON WHICH ORWELL BASED HIS ANIMAL NOVEL.

law of life" (130). Still, the animals hold out hope that some day the wonderful world Old Major had spoken of would arrive.

One summer, Squealer takes the sheep out to a pasture to teach them a new song. For years they had been bleating, "Four legs good, two legs bad." Now they begin to bleat, "Four legs good, two legs better," and the pigs are seen walking about on two legs.

The seven commandments are removed from the barn wall and replaced with a single commandment:

> ALL ANIMALS ARE EQUAL
> BUT SOME ANIMALS ARE MORE EQUAL THAN OTHERS

The pigs supervising the other animals begin to carry whips, and Napoleon begins to appear in human clothes. Other farmers are invited to the farm and sit at the table with the pigs. The white hoof and horn are removed from the flag and the name of the farm is changed back to Manor Farm. The novel ends with the other animals peeking in through the window at the pigs dining with the other farmers, unable to tell which is which.

Historical Parallels in Chapter X

In 1943 Stalin met with Winston Churchill and Franklin D. Roosevelt to join forces against Germany. The first meeting was called the Tehran Conference. Orwell considered fascism as the ultimate realization of capitalism, and therefore saw the affiliation of socialist Russia with the two capitalist countries, England and the United States, as the ultimate betrayal of socialist ideals. This betrayal at the Tehran Conference is portrayed in Animal Farm *with the coming together of the pigs with human farmers. In the end, the differences between pigs and humans disappear.*

THIS IS THE FIRST EDITION DUST JACKET OF A WORK THAT IS NOW IN ITS UMPTEENTH EDITION. IT HAS NEVER GONE OUT OF PRINT.

Chapter 2

George Orwell's *Nineteen Eighty-Four*

Background on the Writing of *Nineteen Eighty-Four*

Nineteen Eighty-Four was Orwell's last and most highly praised novel. Published in 1949 while Orwell was on his deathbed, it is a dark work set in 1984 that describes a world dominated by a totalitarian state. Scholar Denis Donaghue convincingly argues that the novel is a "political fable," a story that warns of the type of world we might all live in if the system of government becomes more important than the people it was meant to serve.

Nineteen Eighty-Four is a dystopian novel. Unlike utopian novels that tell of imaginary worlds where people live in peace and harmony, dystopian novels tell of worlds full of pain, suffering, oppression, and injustice. Psychologist Erich Fromm, in his afterword to the 1961 New American Library edition of the novel, says that *Nineteen Eighty-Four* is "the expression of a mood, and . . . a warning. The mood it expresses is that of near despair about the future of man, and the warning is that unless the course of history changes, men all over the world will lose their most human qualities, will become soulless automatons, and will not even be aware of it."

Like some of the dystopian novels that preceded it, such as Jack London's *The Iron Heel* (1908) and Aldous Huxley's *Brave New World* (1932), *Nineteen Eighty-Four* is full of despair and frightening revelations. Yet, as scholar Herbert Read notes, "Fundamental to Orwell is a *love* of humanity and a passionate desire to live in freedom."

Critic Lionel Trilling credits Orwell's novel for marking a shift in the way people think about economic social systems. He writes:

> The whole effort of the culture of the last hundred years has been directed toward teaching us to understand economic motive as the irrational road to death, and to seek salvation in the rational and the planned. Orwell . . . asks us to consider whether the triumph of certain forces of the mind, in their naked pride and excess, may not produce a state of things far worse than any we have ever known.

Nineteen Eighty-Four warns against the unchecked pursuit of property and power for its own sake and cautions of the world we will create if we place the interests of the state above reason and truth. Many scholars have pointed out that the novel is also a critique of the times in which Orwell lived. In the wake of World War II, Orwell was warning of the horrors that might occur if people did not resist limits being placed on their individual freedom.

Nineteen Eighty-Four tells the story of Winston Smith, a lonely, middle-aged Outer Party worker trapped in a totalitarian world that offers no hope of escape. Smith seeks to gain some sense of hope through his secret relationship with a young woman, but fails to escape the watchful eye of the Party—the political organization that has erased all possibility of privacy (even within one's own mind) in its attempt to retain its power forever.

The Principal Characters in *Nineteen Eighty-Four*

Winston Smith

Winston Smith, the protagonist of the novel, is an Everyman character who represents each of us. Orwell ascribes to the character of Winston the same thoughts,

feelings, suspicions, and desires that each of us might have if we were unfortunate enough to be living in a totalitarian state as cruel and unyielding as Oceania.

Winston is frail and suffers from an ulcer—not the type of man we would typically view as heroic. This is intentional, as Jenni Calder notes when she writes that Winston seems "unremarkable, vulnerable, an ordinary Englishman. . . . Winston's physical frailty emphasizes his ordinariness, and . . . contributes significantly to what Orwell wants us to understand about his hero."

Winston's name is one of the many contrasts in the novel. The first name Winston brings to mind is Winston Churchill, the heroic British prime minister during World War II, which had ended only four years before the book was published. This upper-class name is coupled with "Smith," the most common surname in England, Scotland, Ireland, and the United States. The low is coupled with the high, the privileged with the ordinary, mirroring the tension that threads through the entire novel.

Julia

Julia is Winston's younger lover. She works for the Fiction Department, ironically located in the Ministry of Truth. Unlike Winston, Julia is too young to remember anything before the Party and does not share Winston's desire to know the truth. For Julia, life is simply a matter of appearing to follow the Party line while devising ways around the system. She is more clever than Winston in her ability to arrange meetings away from prying eyes, but her love for Winston and her willingness to accommodate his interest in locating The Brotherhood lead to her capture and psychological conditioning.

Mr. Charrington

Mr. Charrington is the elderly proprietor of the prole (short for "proletariat," or working class) junk shop where Winston bought his diary, and where he buys a

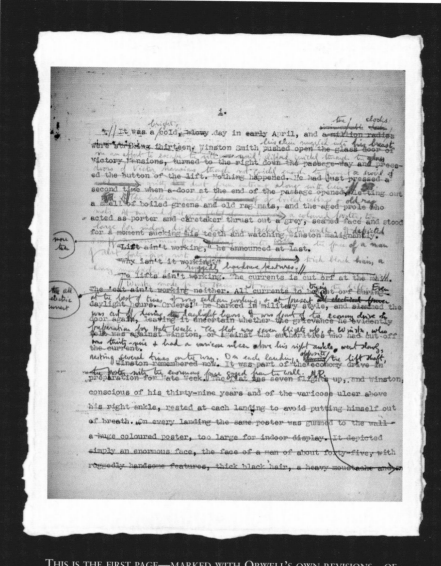

THIS IS THE FIRST PAGE—MARKED WITH ORWELL'S OWN REVISIONS—OF
THE FIRST DRAFT OF *NINETEEN EIGHTY-FOUR*.

coral paperweight and rents a room for himself and Julia. Winston's first impression of Charrington is that the man is "frail and bowed, with a long, benevolent nose, and mild eyes distorted by thick spectacles," with white hair and bushy eyebrows, a man with "a vague air of intellectuality"(80). Later, after Winston discovers that Charrington is actually a member of the Thought Police, he is "not the same person any longer" (185). Charrington's hair is black, he wears no glasses, his eyebrows are no longer bushy, his "body had straightened, and he seemed to have grown bigger" (185); overall, he was cold and alert and appeared to be about thirty-five.

Through Charrington and his betrayal of Smith's confidence, Smith comes to realize that nothing in Oceania is what it appears and no one can be trusted.

O'Brien

Winston simultaneously admires and hates O'Brien, a member of the Inner Party. He is a father figure to Winston, whose own father disappeared when Winston was a small boy, but O'Brien's role as father figure is to reincorporate Winston into the Party. O'Brien appears intelligent and uses twisted logic to "guide" Winston back toward the ideology of the Party; he is controlling Winston even when Winston is not aware of it. Orwell crafts O'Brien so that he not only functions as the source of Winston's suffering, but so he also appears as Winston's savior, inasmuch as he "saves" Winston from thinking freely.

O'Brien represents the totalitarian mindset of the Party, a mindset that rejects the individual and embraces the irrational justifications the Party uses to defend its total domination over Oceania's citizens.

Syme

A comrade of Winston's who works in the Research Department of the Ministry of Truth, Syme is a philologist

(a specialist in the history and use of written and spoken communication) specializing in Newspeak. Syme is working on the compilation of the eleventh edition of the Newspeak dictionary. Orwell describes him as "a tiny creature, smaller than Winston, with dark hair and large, protuberant eyes, at once mournful and derisive" (43). Syme is "venomously orthodox" (44), loyal to the Party, and refers to the "destruction of words" as "a beautiful thing" (45). Syme represents the intellectual, who cannot be tolerated within a totalitarian system without the risk that he or she might reason through the Party's rhetoric and one day speak out against it.

Tom Parsons and Mrs. Parsons

Tom and Mrs. Parsons are Winston's neighbors at Victory Mansions. Tom is thirty-five, chubby, with fair hair and a "froglike face" (49). The Parsons, with their children, represent family life under totalitarian rule. The children are horribly behaved and have the power to turn their parents over to the Thought Police. Mrs. Parsons lives in fear and desperation. Tom Parsons does his best to praise his children for spying and to adhere to the philosophy of the Party. He continues to praise the system even after his own daughter turns him in and he is imprisoned in The Ministry of Love.

Parsons's lack of common sense contrasts with Syme's intellect. Parsons's enthusiasm for the party is fueled by his inability to grasp the dangers their policies present, even to the point where he is unable to see the harm in his own children's horrible behavior.

Martin

Martin is O'Brien's Asian servant. Although O'Brien tells Winston that Martin is "one of us," which Winston assumes to mean that Martin is a member of The Brotherhood, Martin symbolizes the oppression of for-

eigners. He is presumably from Eastasia or Eurasia, the two other major powers in the world. His presence as a servant in the house of an Inner Party member implies that the "enemy" is sometimes pressed into servitude for the benefit of the Party.

Big Brother

Big Brother is the iconic, mythical leader of the Party, and head of Oceania. His face adorns posters and currency and is described several times in the novel. At the end of Part One Winston is staring at Big Brother's face on a coin, a face he describes as "heavy, calm, protecting." Winston wonders "what kind of smile . . . [is] hidden beneath the dark mustache" (87). At the close of Part Three, Winston is staring at Big Brother's face again. Orwell writes, "Forty years it had taken him [Winston] to learn what kind of smile was hidden beneath the dark mustache. O cruel, needless misunderstanding! O stubborn, self-willed exile from the loving breast! Two gin-scented tears trickled down the sides of his [Winston's] nose. But it was all right, everything was all right, the struggle was finished. He had won the victory over himself. He loved Big Brother" (245).

The face of Big Brother has not changed throughout the novel; what has changed is Winston's attitude toward it. Like the Party he symbolizes, Big Brother is constant and unalterable.

Emmanuel Goldstein

Goldstein is the object of all hatred in Oceania. He is the "Enemy of the Party," a former Party member who turned against the Party and now supposedly seeks to destroy everything for which the Party stands. Like Big Brother, he is an invention of the Party and only appears in the novel as an image, a face to which all blame is directed, and may not be a real person. His image is an anti-Semitic

stereotype, "a lean Jewish face, with a great fuzzy aureole of white hair and a small goatee beard—a clever face, and yet somehow inherently despicable, with a kind of senile silliness in the long thin nose near the end of which a pair of spectacles . . . [is] perched. It . . . [resembles] the face of a sheep, and the voice, too, . . . [has] a sheeplike quality" (14). Goldstein is proclaimed to be the author of "a terrible book" full of heresies and is said to command an army of spies and saboteurs who operate in Oceania and who must be rooted out at all costs.

Summary
Part One

Part One of *Nineteen Eighty-Four* establishes the mood of the novel, describing Oceania (one of three powers left in the world), depicting life in London, and introducing Winston Smith and the other key characters. The image is one of a nightmarish world, perpetually at war, where the totalitarian government totally dominates the individual.

Section I.

From the first sentence, *Nineteen Eighty-Four* announces that readers have entered another world, beginning: "It was a bright cold day in April, and the clocks were striking thirteen" (5). Section I of Part One introduces us to the protagonist, Winston Smith, a functionary who works for the Ministry of Truth, a department responsible for changing all records of the past (photographs, newspapers, novels, etc.) to reflect the current claims of the Party.

Winston, like all members of the Party, is constantly under surveillance. The telescreen (which cannot be turned off) in his meager apartment at Victory Mansions transmits propaganda around the clock and keeps him under constant watch with its ability to send and receive images and sound. Helicopters keep watch from the sky. Hidden

microphones listen in on all conversations. And everywhere, on posters and appearing on screens, is the face of Big Brother, the idealized leader of the Party, who is credited with every success the society experiences.

We learn several important details in Section I of Part One:

1. The three slogans of the Party are:

> WAR IS PEACE
> FREEDOM IS SLAVERY
> IGNORANCE IS STRENGTH

2. There are four ministries in the government:

The Ministry of Truth, where Winston works, which concerns itself with "news, entertainment, education, and the fine arts"

The Ministry of Peace, which concerns itself with war

The Ministry of Love, which maintains "law and order," and

The Ministry of Plenty, which is "responsible for economic affairs."

3. We are introduced to Newspeak, a severely abbreviated version of English designed in an absurd attempt to limit, and supposedly eliminate, the ability of any citizen to have a thought that runs counter to the Party line.

4. We learn that it is punishable to think certain thoughts, and Winston Smith lives in constant fear that the "Thought Police" will discover he is

guilty of "thoughtcrime," which could result in him being sent to a labor camp or possibly disappearing—being killed and having every mention of his existence wiped from the records of the past.

Just as the Party has a face, in the form of Big Brother, the "Enemy of the People" (13) has a face in Emmanuel Goldstein, a former leader of the Party who is the object of the daily "Two Minutes Hate," and is blamed for sabotage, treachery, heresy, and betrayal of the Party.

During the Two Minutes Hate described in Section I of Part One, Winston makes note of two other main characters in the novel: Julia, who at this point is referred to as the dark-haired girl from the Fiction Department in the Ministry of Truth, and O'Brien, a member of the Inner Party. Winston suspects that girl might be a member of the Thought Police who is spying on him, but he feels a connection with O'Brien, whom he suspects, like him, questions the "political orthodoxy" (13) of the Party.

Winston's suspicions that the Party may not be the ideal political system are recorded in Winston's diary. He had bought the rare, antique book from a shop, and, in Section I of Part One, he begins to write in it, fully aware that merely opening the book, though not technically illegal, would be punishable by death. The book symbolizes Smith's internal resistance to the Party, and, by the end of the section, he is writing "Down with Big Brother" over and over again in the book, out of view of the watchful telescreen, when someone knocks on his door (19).

Section II.

The knock at the door turns out to be Winston's neighbor, Mrs. Parsons, whose sink is clogged. Her husband, Tom, is away, and she asks Winston to unclog it for her. Winston obliges, which gives us a view of family life under

the totalitarian rule of Ingsoc. The life in the Parsons' apartment is no better than life for Winston. The Parsons children are amateur Thought Police obsessed with finding spies and saboteurs, even to the point where they suspect their own parents, a practice used during the Great Purge in Stalinist Russia where children were compelled to denounce their own parents as disloyal to the Communist Party. Orwell makes it clear that the family unit has broken down. There is no love in the Parsons' household, only deprivation, suspicion, and fear.

"He [Winston] felt as though he were . . . wandering in the forests of the sea bottom, lost in a monstrous world where he himself was the monster. He was alone. The past was dead, the future was unimaginable."
Nineteen Eight-Four, 25

After helping Mrs. Parsons with her clogged plumbing, Winston returns to his apartment where he considers the lonely state of his life. He recalls a dream he had seven years earlier in which someone said to him, "We shall meet in the place where there is no darkness." He attributes the comment to O'Brien, although he cannot remember if he met O'Brien before or after the dream.

In Section II of Part One Orwell sounds the depths of Winston's misery. Winston is alone and notes that he is "already dead" because "thoughtcrime does not entail death: thoughtcrime IS death" (27). And Winston is already guilty of thoughtcrime. He hides his diary, careful to place a bit of dust on the cover so that he will know if anyone finds it.

Section III.

Winston wakes up, recalling a dream in which his mother and infant sister are sinking away from him. He was ten

or eleven when they disappeared, and Winston has the sense that they died so that he could live. The dream ends when he is transported to a bucolic landscape he calls the "Golden Country." There the "girl with the dark hair" (Julia) approaches him across a field. She tears off her clothes, and Winston interprets the gesture as the annihilation "of a whole culture, a whole system of thought, as though Big Brother and the Party and the Thought Police could all be swept into nothingness by a single splendid movement of the arm" (29).

> If all others accepted the lie which the Party imposed—if all records told the same tale—then the lie passed into history and became truth.
> *Nineteen Eighty-Four*, 32

The dream is broken off by a shrill whistle coming from the telescreen in his apartment, waking him for mandatory exercise. While exercising, he thinks about the past, recalling that Airstrip One had once been called England and that Oceania, which is now at war with Eurasia and allied with Eastasia, had only four years earlier been at war with Eastasia and allied with Eurasia. Winston recalls several other memories about the past, such as that the Party did not invent the airplane as they claim and he remembers a time when he held "documentary proof of the falsification of a historical fact" (33).

Section III of Part One accentuates Winston's decline into thoughtcrime. He is recalling the past, the very thing the Party seeks to control. One of the Party slogans is, "Who controls the past . . . controls the future: who controls the present controls the past" (32). The Party's philosophical position is that the past only exists as memories and documentation in the present. Thus, if they can change all documentation and control what people

remember (which they seek to do through "doublethink"), they can effectively control the future and remain in power forever. Because Oceania is presently at war with Eurasia, they claim that they have always been at war with Eurasia. To think otherwise—that is, to remember what actually happened—is thoughtcrime.

Section IV.

Section IV of Part One begins with Winston at work, where he is one of many who must weed through old records and alter them so they reflect what the Party is currently saying happened in the past. Whatever Big Brother says must be made to be "true" by changing any past record that might contradict it. When people "disappear"—when they are captured by the Thought Police and "vaporized"—all record of their existence must be wiped clean.

Winston's "greatest pleasure in life was his work" (39), but as he works his mind is drawn to contradictions between the true past and the alterations he is making.

Section V.

Section V of Part One begins with Winston lunching in the canteen. The mood there, like the mood everywhere in 1984, is dark, fearful, and glum.

Winston is joined by Syme, a comrade who works with Newspeak. Although Syme believes in what he is doing and in the Party, Winston is intrigued by Syme's intellect and fascinated with Syme's work on the Newspeak dictionary, which involves destroying words and limiting language in order to prevent people from thinking thoughts counter to the Party's policies—in order to make thoughtcrime, of which Winston is already guilty,

literally impossible. "The whole climate of thought will be different," Syme explains to Winston. "In fact there will *be* no thought, as we understand it now. Orthodoxy means not thinking—not needing to think. Orthodoxy is unconsciousness" (47).

> Always in your stomach and in your skin there was a sort of protest, a feeling that you had been cheated of something that you had a right to.
> *Nineteen Eighty-Four*, 52

Despite his orthodoxy and his love of Big Brother, Syme, Winston sadly realizes, will ultimately be vaporized, because he "said things that would have been better unsaid . . . read too many books . . . [and] frequented the Chestnut Tree Café," where painters and musicians gathered (49).

The two men are joined by Tom Parsons, who brags about how his little daughter turned a man over to the patrols, claiming he was a spy, based on his shoes. While the men wash down the vile food with Victory gin, a harsh alcoholic beverage used to numb the senses, an announcement from the Ministry of Plenty broadcasts that chocolate rations would be raised to 20 grams a week. Winston recalls that just the day before the Ministry of Plenty had announced that chocolate rations would be *reduced* to 20 grams a week. He is surprised at how easily his comrades fall for the deception, further marking his descent into thoughtcrime.

Section VI.

Section VI of Part One opens with Winston writing in his diary about a visit he made to a prostitute three years earlier. As he writes, he recalls his wife, too—a woman

named Katherine. The marriage, like all marriages in Oceania, had been arranged by the Party in order to produce children. Winston's marriage was loveless and his physical relationship with his wife was routine and unfulfilling. Winston and Katherine had been together for only fifteen months, and he had not seen her for nine to eleven years. Winston does not miss his wife, and seldom thinks of her. He claims that she had "the most stupid, vulgar, empty mind that he had ever encountered" (58).

Orwell's descriptions of Winston's visit to the prostitute and his wife set up Winston's future encounter with Julia. Prior to Julia, Winston's relationships with women were marked by extremes: a bland, loveless marriage and a disgusting sexual encounter with a fifty-year-old woman.

Section VII.

In Section VII of Part One, we discover that 85 percent of the population of Oceania is made up of proles. The proles are the lowest of the three strata of society. Above them is the Outer Party, to which Winston belongs, followed by the Inner Party, to which O'Brien belongs. The proles are the worker ants in Orwell's imagined world. They scrape out a meager living on the outskirts of Winston's circle. The Party considers them too inferior to represent any threat to the Party's power. The proles take no interest in politics and believe whatever the Party tells them. Nevertheless, Winston sees them as the only hope for a better world. If the proles could be organized into a rebellion against the Party, the Party could be overthrown. But the system the Party has in place does not allow enough latitude for the proles to become aware enough to mount any resistance to the Party.

Section VII of Part One also provides specifics about the "documentary proof of the falsification of a historical fact" that was mentioned in Section III of Part One. Three men—Jones, Aaronson, and Rutherford—had been among the last of those left after Goldstein fled. They had been captured and forced to confess to all manner of crimes against the Party. Afterward, Winston had seen them together at the Chestnut Tree Café (which foreshadows Winston's own future at the end of the novel). Their presence in public was not a reprieve, but part of the workings of the Party, which only executed Party members after they had been reincorporated into the system.

> They were born, they passed through a brief blossoming period of beauty and sexual desire, they married at twenty, they were middle-aged at thirty, they died, for the most part, at sixty. Heavy physical work, the care of home and children, petty quarrels with neighbors, films, football, beer, and, above all, gambling filled up the horizon of their minds. To keep them in control was not difficult.
> *Nineteen Eighty-Four*, 61–62

This avoided the possibility of someone becoming a martyr. Five years after the three men were arrested again, a piece of newsprint came across Winston's desk. The piece of paper had a photograph of the three men at a Party function in New York and was dated the same time that the three men were, according to their confessions, supposed to be on Eurasian soil. The photograph was physical proof that their confessions were lies. Winston destroyed the slip of newspaper by dropping it down a "memory hole" where it would be incinerated, but he is still thinking about it, which means that the Party does not yet have full control over his memory.

Winston is interested in discovering the truth, and his thoughts have led him farther into thoughtcrime. Section VII of Part One ends with Winston writing:

> Freedom is the freedom to say that two plus two make four. If that is granted, all else follows.
> *Nineteen Eighty-Four*, 69

Section VIII.

Convinced that the only hope lies with the proles and in the search for truth, Winston walks into the "labyrinth of London" (70) where the proles live. Instead of finding the last hope of humanity, he finds people obsessed with the lottery (one way the Party keeps the proles distracted). At one point he encounters an elderly man and buys him a beer in a pub. The man is old enough to recall life before the revolution, but his mind is so addled he is unable to verify for Winston whether the Party's stories about the past are true or fabrications.

Winston's wanderings lead him back to the junk shop where he bought the diary. He is attracted to a glass paperweight with a bit of coral in its center, because it is an object that serves no function other than its beauty. Mr. Charrington, the shop's proprietor, shows him to a room with several other items: a bed, a photograph of a church bolted to the wall, a chair, and so on. No telescreen is there and Winston gets the idea that Mr. Charrington might be persuaded to rent the room for a few dollars a week.

Intent on returning to the shop, Winston exits and passes the girl with the dark hair (Julia) in the street. Convinced that she is following him, he fantasizes about following her and smashing in her head so that she cannot report him to the Thought Police or turn him over to the patrols. Unable to bring himself to kill her, mainly because

he cannot figure out how to safely accomplish the task, he returns home, where he steadies himself with Victory gin and considers the horrors of being arrested by the Thought Police—the torture and pain that inevitably lead to confession. And he thinks of O'Brien and the phrase, "We shall meet in the place where there is no darkness," which he is sure means the "imagined future" (87).

Section VIII and Part One end with Winston alone in his room staring at the face of Big Brother, recalling the three maxims: war is peace, freedom is slavery, and ignorance is strength.

Part Two

Part Two concerns itself with the relationship between Winston Smith and Julia. The romance that emerges between Winston and Julia is a dark and foreboding one, set against a horrific background. It accentuates Winston's individual humanity and highlights the inhumanity of the totalitarian state—a place where even love is forbidden. Part One establishes the world in which Winston and Julia meet, and Part Two details the relationship between the two.

Section I.

Part Two opens four days after Winston sights Julia outside the junk shop in the proles section of London. He is on his way to the restroom when he sees "the girl with dark hair" approaching from the other end of the corridor, her right arm in a sling. When she stumbles and falls to the ground, he is torn between his fear that she is his enemy and his concern for a fellow human being—an emotion that shows how far away from the Party line he has strayed.

As Winston helps her up, she slips a note into his hand. Expecting the note to contain some threat, he is terrified. Under the watchful eyes of the government, he is unable to safely examine the note for eight minutes. When he does get a chance to read the note in secret, he discovers, to his shock, that the note reads, "I Love You" (90).

He is stunned and excited. It takes him a week to figure out a way to meet with her. Finally, during lunch, he inconspicuously manages to sit at her table in the canteen. They arrange to meet at Victory Square near the monument. When Winston arrives, he locates her but can only approach her after a crowd gathers to watch a passing group of Eurasian prisoners. Using the crowd as cover, Winston manages to get next to Julia, but they avoid eye contact for fear they will be discovered, and are only able to hold hands for ten seconds without risking someone seeing them. Eyes forward, staring at the passing prisoners, Julia gives him directions to a place in the woods a half an hour away by train, where they agree to meet on Sunday afternoon.

Section II.

Winston meets Julia, whose name he finally learns, in the woods. Both are careful not to speak where there may be hidden microphones. Winston is self-conscious about his age and the poor condition of his body. He is thirty-nine and has varicose veins. She is only twenty-six, but she says she does not care about the differences in either their ages or their bodies. She explains that she was attracted to Winston because she could tell he opposed the Party (particularly the Inner Party), and she tells him that she has been to the spot many times with many men, which pleases Winston. Chastity is revered by the Party, and Winston opposes anything the Party supports. They make

love, but the act is not one of romantic passion. Orwell writes, "you could not have pure love or pure lust nowadays. No emotion was pure, because everything was mixed up with fear and hatred. Their embrace had been a battle, the climax a victory. It was a blow struck against the Party. It was a political act" (105). Afterward, they doze.

> He looked up. It was the girl. She shook her head, evidently as a warning that he must keep silent, then parted the bushes and quickly led the way along the narrow track into the wood.
> *Nineteen Eighty-Four*, 99

Section III.

When they awake, Julia takes the lead in planning future meetings. During the remainder of the month, they only manage to meet once, in the belfry of a ruined church.

Julia, like Winston, outwardly appears to follow the Party rules, volunteering her time in preparation for celebrations, such as Hate Week, and working for the Anti-Sex League, when she actually despises the Party. Her actions are a means of avoiding detection and facilitate her diversions from Party policy, such as her affair with Winston.

The Party position is straightforward: it opposes close emotional relationships of any kind. It encourages parents to care for their children only for the purposes of child care (and it has plans to one day eliminate even this basic emotional need), and it encourages children to spy on their parents. The Party opposes any form of sex that brings pleasure or emotional bonding, and advocates sex only for procreation. "Duty to the Party," they call it (110).

The end of Section III of Part Two hints at the differences between Julia and Winston. Julia, Orwell writes,

"was very young . . . she still expected something from life" (112). Winston realizes that their actions (and thoughts) have already doomed them, and they are living on borrowed time. "We are the dead," he tells her (113). But Julia insists that she is alive.

Section IV.

In Section IV of Part Two Winston has rented the room above Mr. Charrington's junk shop and outfitted it as best he can with cooking materials and meager supplies. The coral paperweight is on the table. When Julia comes, she brings real coffee that she has purchased from the black market. Outside the window a large middle-aged prole woman hangs laundry and sings a sentimental song created by the Party to pacify the workers.

> As he sat waiting on the edge of the bed he thought again of the cellars of the Ministry of Love. It was curious how that predestined horror moved in and out of one's consciousness. There it lay, fixed in future time, preceding death as surely as 99 precedes 100.
> *Nineteen Eighty-Four*, 116

Winston feels happy, though he realizes how foolish renting the room was, and that such a rash action is sure to hasten their discovery by the Thought Police and their eventual torture and vaporization.

When a rat peaks out from behind some loose boards, Winston is terrified, and we learn that rats are his greatest fear, foreshadowing Winston's later visit to Room 101.

Section V.

Winston's comrade, Syme, disappears, as Winston suspected he would. Few people mention his absence. Meanwhile,

the room above Charrington's shop, despite its squalor, has become a paradise for Winston. He continues to daydream about a prole revolution and fantasizes about locating and joining an organization called The Brotherhood, a group of Goldstein followers rumored to be secreted among the Party members. Julia does not share his passion for revolution but relishes their times together. "I am not interested in the next generation, dear," she tells him. "I am interested in *us*" (129).

The room itself becomes for Winston a rebellious act. The fact that the room could exist, that they had apparently succeeded in setting it up and meeting there, means that the Party was not all-powerful. If it was possible to resist them in this small way, Winston realized, it was possible to resist them in other ways as well, and maybe to defeat them one day. The renting of the room also places Winston closer to the proles, in whom Winston believes the fate of the world rests and with whom he hopes to align himself in order to organize an overthrow of the Party.

Section VI.

Section VI of Part Two is a turning point for Winston. O'Brien confronts him in the hallway of the Ministry of Truth. He claims to have read some of Winston's Newspeak articles in the newspaper. He gives Winston his home address under the pretense of lending him a current copy of the Newspeak dictionary. Winston is excited and interprets the gesture as a possible entry into the Brotherhood.

Section VII.

Winston wakes up next to Julia in the room above the junk shop. He is weeping. In his sleep he recalled his childhood, which he recounts to Julia. He remembers the

constant hunger and how he would badger his mother for more than his share of the food. The last time he saw his mother and infant sister, his mother had brought home two ounces of chocolate. After haranguing her to give him two-thirds, he decides he should have it all, snatches the third his mother had given his ailing sister, and runs from the apartment. When he returns, his mother and sister are gone. He never sees them again.

The memory of his selfishness stirs in him a realization that "what mattered were individual relationships, and [that] a completely helpless gesture, an embrace, a tear, a word spoken to a dying man, could have value in itself" (136). The dream shows that Smith is beginning to regain emotions that he had lost.

The section ends with Winston pointing out to Julia that once they are captured, they will inevitably confess, but they must never betray each other; they must never stop loving one another.

Section VIII.

Encouraged by O'Brien's invitation in Section VI of Part Two, Winston visits O'Brien's home. He brings Julia, which he knows is "sheer folly" (138). If Winston is wrong about O'Brien, he is sealing his fate with the visit.

To Winston's astonishment O'Brien turns off the telescreen in his office. Winston pours out everything he had been thinking recently about The Brotherhood and resistance to the Party. O'Brien assures him that The Brotherhood is real and that he and his servant, Martin, are members. Over a glass of wine O'Brien quizzes Winston about what he is willing to do for The Brotherhood. Winston says he is willing to die, to murder, to commit suicide, to throw acid in a child's face, and so on, but when O'Brien asks if Winston and Julia are willing to separate and never see each other again, Julia pipes in, saying, "No." Winston agrees. They are not

prepared to give up their relationship even to bring an end to the Party.

O'Brien explains that members of The Brotherhood are "the dead," and that, in joining the group, Winston and Julia are turning their lives over for the benefit of the future. He tells Winston that one day soon, Winston should leave his briefcase at home. Someone will approach him and ask if he dropped his briefcase, and hand him a similar case. Inside will be a copy of Goldstein's book.

Section IX.

The book is delivered to Winston by a stranger on the street, but Winston must delay reading it. Hate Week keeps him busy ninety hours a week. On the sixth day of Hate Week it is announced that they are actually at war with Eastasia and allied with Eurasia, which means that now everyone is to believe that they have always been at war with Eastasia. Winston and other members in the Party have to go back through all earlier references to a war with Eurasia and change them. When the workload lessens, Winston finally has an opportunity to visit the room above Charrington's shop and open the book he had received from a man on the street.

Section IX of Part Two includes excerpts from Chapter 1, titled "Ignorance is Strength," and Chapter 3, titled "War is Peace," of Goldstein's book. Mostly, the book confirms what Winston already suspects. For the reader of *Nineteen Eight-Four* these excerpts explain the historical precedence and philosophical theories underlying the oppressive political structure of the world.

> There was truth and there was untruth, and if you clung to the truth even against the whole world, you were not mad.
> *Nineteen Eighty-Four*, 179

The following points are brought out in Goldstein's book:

> Throughout history, "there have been three kinds of people": the high, the middle, and the low. The goal of the high has always been to remain in power. The goal of the middle has always been to rise up and take over from the high. The goal of the low is "to abolish all distinctions and create a society in which all men shall be equal." (166)

The middle takes over from the high by enlisting "the low on their side by pretending to them that they are fighting for liberty and justice" (166). Once they have achieved the high position, they keep the low in the same place they have always occupied.

The three political movements running the world now—Ingsoc in Oceania, Neo-Bolshevism in Eurasia, and Death-worship in Eastasia—all share "the conscious aim of perpetuating unfreedom and inequality" (167). Human equality is "no longer an ideal to be striven after, but a danger to be averted" (168). Each is a totalitarian state, efficiently run to eliminate any chance of rebellion from the low and middle segments of society by making impossible the "four ways in which a ruling group can fall from power" (170):

1. Someone outside takes the ruling group from power,
2. the ruling group governs "so inefficiently that the masses are stirred to revolt,"
3. the ruling group "allows a strong and discontented Middle Group to come into being,"
4. the ruling group "loses its own self-confidence and willingness to govern." (170)

If a ruling group can effectively eliminate these four threats, they can remain in power indefinitely. All four are dealt with in the following manner:

1. Because the world has formed into three geographically large and powerful regions—Oceania, Eastasia, and Eurasia—no one region has the power to overthrow another. The only way one could lose its power is gradually over time, and each can easily protect itself from a slow erosion of its power.

2. The "masses never revolt of their own accord" (171). As long as they are kept busy with production and provided no alternative lifestyle against which they might measure their own as oppressed, they will remain no threat to the ruling power.

3. The ruling power can prevent a "discontented Middle Group" from forming by keeping the population under constant surveillance and controlling every aspect of their lives, including what and how they think.

4. There isp no danger of the ruling group losing its willingness to be the ruling group.

Thus, the most important ongoing concern, if the ruling group wants to retain power indefinitely, is to guard against anyone in the middle group from becoming strong. The ruling group has several strategies in place for assuring that the masses remain passive and weak:

1. The Party owns all real property, thus no one can develop a desire to possess more, because no one can own anything other than personal possessions.

2. The world is kept in perpetual war so that the workers are kept busy, constantly producing products that the military conflict consumes.

3. Big Brother is created as a focus for the population's "love, fear, and reverence" (171). Similarly, Goldstein is created as the focus of their loathing.

4. Nothing can be passed down to children.

5. The Proletariat (proles) are not allowed to rise into the Inner or Outer Party. Proles who are ambitious are simply eliminated by the Thought Police.

6. Outer Party members who are ambitious are allowed to rise up into the Inner Party, thus preventing them from growing dissatisfied and rebellious.

7. All Party members are kept under surveillance from the moment they are born until the moment they die.

8. There are no laws, and when members are arrested, tortured, imprisoned, or executed, it is never for an identifiable crime.

9. Party members have no lives independent of the party; they are kept in a frenzied state involving unwavering loyalty toward the Party and hatred for the enemy.

10. Party members are expected to believe in the infallibility of the Party, which requires them to engage in *doublethink*. Doublethink is the ability to hold "two contradictory beliefs in one's mind simultaneously, and . . . [accept] both of them" (176). Doublethink involves a person engaging in "conscious deception while retaining the firmness of purpose that goes with complete honesty. To tell deliberate lies while genuinely believing in them, to forget any fact that has become inconvenient, and then, when it becomes necessary again, to draw it back from oblivion for just so long as it is needed, to deny the existence of objective reality and all the while to take account of the reality which one denies" (177).

11. The ruling party controls the past (assuring, for example, that the Party has always been right about everything), by controlling how the past is remembered. If everyone believes that Oceania has always been at war with Eurasia, then in the absence of any objective evidence—as far as the human mind is concerned—Oceania has always been at war with Eurasia.

When Winston pauses from his reading, he discovers that Julia has fallen asleep again.

Section X.

Winston and Julia wake up in the room above Charrington's shop. Outside, the heavy-set prole woman is singing and hanging laundry. They stand at the window together. The world seems to have been washed clean, and Winston considers how Eurasia, Eastasia, and Oceania all

THIS MOVIE POSTER OF *NINETEEN EIGHTY-FOUR* SHOWS ITS MOST FRIGHTENING IMAGE AND SLOGAN.

see the same sky, how birds and proles sing, though the Party does not sing. He realizes that he and Julia will not benefit from any actions they might make resisting the Party, but the proles will benefit. Their efforts are for the future. "We are the dead," they remark, gazing out the window (182).

"You are the dead," an "iron voice" says (182). They are shocked. Behind the picture on the wall was a hidden telescreen. They had been under surveillance the entire time. The room fills with men in black suits. They smash the coral paperweight, an act symbolizing the destruction of the private world Winston and Julia have made. The men violently restrain Winston and Julia, then Mr. Charrington enters the room and Winston realizes that the shopkeeper is a member of the Thought Police.

Part Three

Part Three resolves Winston and Julia's tragic love story, recounting events after Winston is captured, and balancing the novel by reestablishing the world introduced in Part One. The novel adheres to the following pattern:

Part One: Describes the oppressive totalitarian world where the individual, represented by Winston Smith, cannot exist, and love is impossible.

Part Two: Tracks Winston's love affair with Julia, his attempts to assert his individuality, and his efforts to challenge the uniformity of the Party.

Part Three: Reveals that events in Part Two were not as they seemed and that Winston's affair with Julia and his attempt to locate The Brotherhood had occurred under the ever-watchful eye of the Party. In a world where totalitarian

oppression is absolute, love cannot endure.

Section I.

Part Three opens with Winston starving in the brightly lit rooms of the Ministry of Love. Telescreens are everywhere, watching. The holding cell where Winston is first placed is noisy and smelly. There is nothing to eat. No clocks. No windows. Members of the Party are mixed with "ordinary criminals." Only the "Party prisoners . . . [are] silent and terrified." Here Winston first hears whispers about Room 101.

Winston wonders if O'Brien has been arrested, too, and if someone will be sending him a razor blade so he can commit suicide and avoid the torture to which he is otherwise sure to be subjected.

The lights are never turned out and Winston realizes that he is in "the place with no darkness," about which he had dreamed. He encounters a poet named Ampleforth, who suspects he has been arrested for keeping the word God in a poem by Kipling. He also encounters his neighbor, Parsons, whose little daughter turned him in for talking in his sleep. The Party members are eventually separated from the proles. They are beaten, starved, humiliated, and occasionally dragged off, screaming, to Room 101.

It was easier to confess everything and implicate everybody. Besides, in a sense it was all true. It was true that he had been the enemy of the Party, and in the eyes of the Party there was no distinction between the thought and the deed.
Nineteen Eighty-Four, 200

Section I of Part Three ends when O'Brien enters the room. At first Winston suspects that O'Brien has been arrested, but he quickly realizes that O'Brien is part of the process—he has always been part of the process. The guard with O'Brien smashes Winston's left elbow with a truncheon and Winston falls to the ground in pain.

Section II.

Winston wakes strapped to a board, unable to move. He cannot recall how many beatings and interrogations, or how much torture he has already endured, but he confesses to everything of which he is accused, real or imagined. He confesses to being in league with Goldstein for years and to being a paid spy for Eastasia for the past sixteen years. He confesses to murdering his wife and everything else of which they accuse him.

O'Brien enters and tells Winston that he has been watching him for seven years, ever since Winston dreamed of a voice telling him, "We shall meet in the place where there is no darkness" (201). Winston now recognizes the dream voice as O'Brien's.

Winston is hooked up to a machine that causes insufferable pain. The machine is under O'Brien's control. O'Brien tests the machine at a setting of forty and tells Winston that the machine goes to one hundred. If Winston lies during O'Brien's interrogation, O'Brien will activate the machine.

O'Brien questions Winston about issues related to memory, not reality. At one point he holds up the slip of newspaper with the picture of Jones, Aaronson, and Rutherford and tells him that the photograph does not exist. O'Brien expresses the basic philosophy of the Party, that there is no objective reality, only what lies in the mind. If one believes something, then it is true. O'Brien explains:

Only the disciplined mind can see reality, Winston. You believe that reality is something objective, external, existing in its own right. You also believe that the nature of reality is self-evident. When you delude yourself into thinking that you see something, you assume that everyone else sees the same thing as you. But I tell you, Winston, that reality is not external. Reality exists in the human mind, and nowhere else. Not in the individual mind, which can make mistakes, and in any case soon perishes; only in the mind of the Party, which is collective and immortal. Whatever the Party holds to be truth *is* truth.
Nineteen Eighty-Four, 205

Using the machine to inflict pain, O'Brien reconditions Winston to believe what the Party believes. At one point, he says that if the party claims two plus two is sometimes five, then that is true. He holds up four fingers and asks Winston how many he sees. When Winston insists that he sees four, he is punished. When he says he sees five, O'Brien knows he is lying, and he is punished. Eventually, Winston is suffering so much he actually cannot tell how many fingers O'Brien is holding, which O'Brien considers an improvement.

In Section II of Part Three O'Brien explains to Winston that the Party will tolerate no martyrs. Every thought criminal must be reconditioned into a faithful member of the Party before he or she is executed so there is no chance that others will look up to them and use them as objects to nurture the seeds of rebellion.

At the close of Section II O'Brien allows Winston to ask questions. When he asks about Julia, O'Brien tells him

that Julia betrayed him, "immediately—unreservedly" (213).

Section III.

Winston is again strapped to the board and wired to O'Brien's machine, but his binds are looser as a result of his partial reconditioning. O'Brien explains to Winston that there are three stages to his "reintegration": learning, understanding, and acceptance (215). Winston has already passed the first stage and is now entering into understanding.

O'Brien admits he wrote Goldstein's book and tells Winston that the idea of a proletarian revolt is nonsense. The Party is forever. He explains that the Party seeks power solely for its own sake. They are not ruling for the good of the people, for wealth, for long life, or for happiness, "only power, pure power" (217). The power O'Brien is talking about is a collective power. It does not rest with individuals. "The individual," O'Brien further explains, "only has power in so far as he ceases to be an individual" (218). On his own, the individual is always defeated, but if he completely submits to the Party, he becomes the Party, and thereby becomes "all-powerful and immortal" (218). This is what is meant by "Freedom is Slavery," and its reverse, "Slavery is Freedom."

In Section III of Part Three, Orwell, through O'Brien, defines the totalitarian world of the Party as the opposite of a utopia—as a dystopia, one that fills everyone forever with the "thrill of victory, the sensation of trampling on an enemy who is helpless" (220). "If you want a picture of the future," O'Brien tells Winston, "imagine a boot stamping on a human face—forever" (220).

To force Winston into realizing how alone and powerless he is, O'Brien makes him strip and stand before a mirror. Winston is horrified by the emaciated person he

has become. He is filthy. His hair and teeth are falling out. O'Brien points out to Winston that his mind is in the same condition as his body; he has betrayed everyone he has known and everything in which he once believed. But when asked if he can think of "a single degradation that has not happened" to him, Winston reminds O'Brien that he has not betrayed Julia, because, as O'Brien realizes, he has not stopped loving her, despite having betrayed her in confessions.

Section IV.

Winston is alone in his room within the Ministry of Love. He has capitulated, and as a result they have allowed him to bathe and have been feeding him. Already his strength is returning. His mind is nearly in line with the Party. When he writes the thoughts in his head, they match the Party line. He writes: "Freedom is Slavery," "Two Plus Two Makes Five," and "God is Power" (228). But then his thoughts are interrupted by his memory of the Golden Country and his time with Julia. He is horrified when he screams out, "Julia! Julia! Julia, my love! Julia!" (230). He imagines that he might be able to fool them long enough so that they will shoot him and in the moment before he dies he can fill his mind with hatred for Big Brother. Then, he reasons, he will have won some victory against their attempts to fully control his mind. But O'Brien is aware of Winston's thoughts and orders him to Room 101.

Section V.

In Room 101 Winston encounters what everyone encounters in Room 101—"the worst thing in the world" (233). For Winston, that is rats. O'Brien has a cage attached to Winston's face. At the other end of the cage are several large, hungry rats. When the last lever is pressed, the rats

will have access to Winston's face.

The thought of being consumed by rats is too much for Winston to take. He breaks down and screams, "Do it to Julia!" In the end Winston has succumbed and betrayed even his love for Julia.

The Party has won.

Section VI.

Winston has been reintegrated back into the Outer Party. He has a job of no consequence and spends time at The Chestnut Café drinking Victory Gin, tracing "2 + 2 = 5" in the dust on the tables, and shambling through his daily affairs. He has difficulty keeping his mind on one subject for very long, but it no longer matters. When he chances upon Julia in the street one day, they both admit to betraying each other, but there is neither love nor regret in their exchange. The past is gone forever. Winston's mind is no longer capable of thoughtcrime. It is barely capable of thought. The novel closes with him staring reverently at a picture of Big Brother, who, in the end, he finally loves, but only after his mind has been wholly destroyed.

Appendix—The Principles of Newspeak

Nineteen Eighty-Four, at Orwell's insistence, contains an appendix, which describes the basics of Newspeak. The absurdity of Newspeak exposes the idiocy of totalitarian strategies for control and shows the illogical lengths to which totalitarian states would go to limit individual freedom, control the population, and retain power.

The section points out that Newspeak falls into three categories:

The A Vocabulary: "Words needed for business and everyday life," such as "hit, run, dog, tree" (247).

The B Vocabulary: "Words . . . deliberately constructed for political purposes," such as "good-think," "crimethink," "bellyfeel" and "Ingsoc" (249-250).

The C Vocabulary: Words consisting "entirely of scientific and technical terms" (254).

Orwell ends the appendix by pointing out that the opening to the Declaration of Independence, which begins, "We hold these truths to be self-evident that all men are created equal . . . etc," would, in Newspeak, all be encompassed in the single word "crimethink" (256).

Final Words

George Orwell considered *Nineteen Eighty-Four* a satire, but the target of his satire was not socialism or the British Labor Party, as some early reviewers claimed; rather, his target was the corruption and abuse of power he saw within governments and political organizations. Orwell says that he intended *Nineteen Eighty-Four* as "a show-up of the perversions to which a centralized economy is liable and which have already been partly realized in Communism and Fascism." His primary concern was the erosion of individual human rights by economic and political forces.

Orwell did not believe the totalitarian world of the novel would "necessarily . . . arrive," but he did claim that "something resembling it could arrive." He said: "I believe also that totalitarian ideas have taken root in the minds of intellectuals everywhere, and I have tried to draw these ideas out to their logical conclusions." The most horrifying part of the message that Orwell relays in *Nineteen Eighty-Four* is not the nightmarish world he describes, but his claim that "totalitarianism, if not fought against, could triumph anywhere." No country is immune. No population of people is completely safe.

Chronology

1903   Eric Blair is born on June 25 in Motihari, Bengal.

1904   Moves back to England with his mother, Ida, and his sister, Marjorie.

1908   His sister, Avril, is born.

1911   Enters St. Cyprian's, a private boarding school.

1912   His father retires and returns to England from India.

1914   Meets and becomes friends with the Buddicom children, Jacintha, Prosper, and Guinever.
Publishes poem "Awake! Young Men of England" in the *Henley and South Oxfordshire Standard*.

1916   Takes exam for college, but comes in fourteenth—too low for admittance to Eton.
Publishes poem "Kitchener" in the *Henley and South Oxfordshire Standard*.
In December he leaves St. Cyprian's.

1917   Spends one semester at Wellington College, then enters Eton College as a King's Scholar in May.

1918   Publishes pieces in student journal, the *Election Times*.

1920   Publishes pieces in *College Days*.

1921   Completes education at Eton and moves to Southwold, England, to stay with his parents.

1922   Joins Indian Imperial Police and travels to Mandalay, Burma, under appointment as probationary assistant superintendent of police.

1924   Completes training school and is posted to district headquarters in Myaungmya, and then to Twante

as subdivisional police officer, followed by a post in Syriam, where he is assistant district superintendent.

1925 Transfers to Insein, Burma, as head of district headquarters.

1926 Transfers to Moulmein, Burma, then to Katha, where he contracts dengue fever.

1927 In July he is granted an eight-month medical leave and travels back to Southwold after a brief stopover in Marseilles, France.

In October he begins tramping expeditions and works on his writing.

In November he resigns from the Imperial Police to pursue a career as a writer.

1928 Moves to Left Bank in Paris and works on early versions of *Down and Out in Paris and London* and *Burmese Days*.

In October he publishes his first professional writing, "La Censure en Angleterre," in literary journal *Le Monde*.

Sells pieces to *Progrés Civique* and *GK's Weekly*.

Coughs up blood and spends several weeks in the public ward at Hôpital Cochin.

1929 Publishes writing in *Progrés Civique* and *Adelphi*. In December he returns to Southwold.

1930 Continues tramping expeditions.

1932 Takes teaching position at The Hawthorns, a private boys' school.

Literary agent, Leonard Moore, places *Down and Out in Paris and London* with publisher Victor Gollancz.

1933 Gollancz publishes *Down and Out in Paris and London* under the pseudonym George Orwell at Blair's request. Harper & Brothers publishes American edition in June.

Takes position teaching French at Frays College.

1934   *Burmese Days* is published in America.

1935   *Burmese Days* is published in England.

A Clergyman's Daughter is published in England.

1936   Travels to North England to research book on working-class life.

In April he rents a former village shop in Wallington, Hertfordshire.

A Clergyman's Daughter is published in America.

Marries Eileen O'Shaughnessy on June 9.

Keep the Aspidistra Flying is published in England.

In December he travels to Spain, where he enlists in the Workers' Party of Marxist Unification (Partido Obrero de Unificación Marxista; POUM) to fight against fascism.

1937   *The Road to Wigan Pier* is published.

Eileen travels to Spain to be near Orwell.

In May he is shot in the neck by a sniper.

He is discharged from the POUM in June in hopes of joining the International Brigade.

POUM is declared illegal; Orwell and Eileen narrowly escape Spain and return to England.

1938   In March he begins coughing up blood and is sent to Preston Hall Sanatorium for six months; it is suspected that he has tuberculosis.

Homage to Catalonia is published.

In July Orwell and Eileen travel to Marrakech in French Morocco.

1939   Returns to shop in Wallington.

Coming Up for Air is published.

On June 28 his father dies.

1940   Begins a weekly theater column for *Time and Tide*.

In June Eileen's brother is killed in the war.

Inside the Whale and Other Essays is published.

1941   Begins writing "London Letter" column for *Partisan Review*.
        In August he joins the British Broadcasting Corporation (BBC), preparing shows for broadcast in India to support the war effort.
        The Lion and the Unicorn: Socialism and the English Genius is published.

1943   Quits position with the BBC and becomes the literary editor of the *Tribune*.

1944   In June Orwell and Eileen adopt a baby boy, Richard Horatio Blair.

1945   Quits position as literary editor of the *Tribune*.
        Visits Germany and France as a war correspondent for the *Observer*.
        Animal Farm is published by Secker and Warburg.
        On March 29, Eileen dies of heart failure after a bad reaction to anesthesia.

1946   Moves to Barnhill on Scottish island of Jura.
        Critical Essays is published by Secker and Warburg.
        James Burnham and the Managerial Revolution is published by Socialist Book Centre.
        American version of *Critical Essays*, titled *Dickens, Dali, and Others*, is published by Reynal & Hitchcock.
        American version of *Animal Farm* published by Harcourt Brace.

1947   Visits London, where he adapts *Animal Farm* for BBC radio program.
        Breaks long-term publishing agreement with Victor Gollancz.
        Toward the end of the year, Orwell becomes increasingly ill, and on December 24 he is admitted for a long stay at Hairmyres Hospital.

1948   Spends half the year in the hospital while completing *Nineteen Eighty-Four.*

1949   Gets ill again and must be hospitalized; is admitted to Cotswold Sanatorium in January.

Nineteen Eighty-Four is published.

In September he is moved to University College Hospital.

On October 13 he marries Sonia Brownell while he is still in the hospital.

1950   Dies of tuberculosis in the hospital on January 21.

Works

Novels
Burmese Days. New York: Harper, 1934.
A Clergyman's Daughter. London: Gollancz, 1935.
Keep the Aspidistra Flying. London: Gollancz, 1936.
Coming Up for Air. London: Gollancz, 1939. Curly,
Animal Farm. London: Secker and Warburg, 1945.
Nineteen Eighty-Four. New York: Harcourt, 1949.

Creative Nonfiction Books
Down and Out in Paris and London. New York: Harper, 1933.
The Road to Wigan Pier. London: Gollancz, 1937.
Homage to Catalonia. London: Secker and Warburg, 1938.

General Nonfiction Books
The English People. London: Collins, 1947.

Collections of Essays and Articles
Inside the Whale, and Other Essays. London: Gollancz, 1940.
The Lion and the Unicorn: Socialism and the English Genius. London: Secker & Warburg, 1941.
Critical Essays. London: Secker and Warburg, 1946.
James Burnham and the Managerial Revolution. London: Socialist Book Centre, 1946.
Dickens, Dali, and Others (American version of *Critical Essays*). London: Reynal & Hitchcock, 1946.

Shooting an Elephant, and Other Essays. New York: Harcourt, 1950.

Such, Such Were the Joys. New York: Harcourt, 1953, published as *England Your England, and Other Essays* (abridged edition). London: Secker and Warburg, 1953.

Selected Essays. New York: Penguin, 1957.

Collected Essays. London: Secker, 1961.

Decline of the English Murder & Other Essays. New York: Penguin, 1965.

The Collected Essays, Journalism, and Letters of George Orwell. Edited by Sonia Orwell and Ian Angus. Four volumes: Vol. 1, *An Age Like This: 1920–1940*, Vol. 2, *My Country Right or Left: 1940–1943*, Vol. 3, *As I Please: 1943–1945*, and Vol. 4, *In Front of Your Nose: 1945–1950*. New York: Harcourt, 1968.

The Penguin Complete Longer Non-Fiction of George Orwell (omnibus volume). Harmondsworth, England: Penguin, 1983.

The Penguin Essays of George Orwell. Harmondsworth, England: Penguin, 1984.

Orwell: The Lost Writings. Edited by W. J. West. New York: Arbor House, 1985.

Orwell: The War Broadcasts. Edited by W. J. West. London: Duckworth/British Broadcasting Corp., 1985. Published as *Orwell: The War Commentaries*, New York: Pantheon, 1986.

Other Collected Works

The Orwell Reader. New York: Harcourt Brace, 1956.

The Works. 14 vols. London: Secker and Warburg, 1986.

Selected Writings. New York: Heinemann, 1957.

The Complete Works of George Orwell. 20 vols. Edited by Peter Davison. London: Secker and Warburg, 1998.

The Penguin Complete Novels of George Orwell (omnibus volume). New York: Penguin, 1983.

Filmography

1984. BBC Sunday Night Theatre. (TV). Dir. Rudolph
Cartier.
Screenplay by Nigel Kneale. 1954.
Animal Farm. Dir. Joy Batchelor and John Halas.
Screenplay by Joy Batchelor, Joseph Bryan, John
Halas, Borden Mace, Philip Stapp, and Lothar Wolff.
1954.
1984. Dir. Michael Anderson. Screenplay by Ralph
Gilbert Bettison and William Templeton. 1955.
The Road to Wigan Pier. (TV). Dir. Frank Cvitanovich.
1973.
A Clergyman's Daughter. Dir. Alvin Rakoff. Screenplay
by John Peacock. 1983.
1984. Dir. Michael Radford. Screenplay by Michael
Radford. 1984.
George Orwell: Great Writers of the Twentieth Century.
(TV Documentary). Based on the life and work of
George Orwell. Clark TV Productions. 1996.
Keep the Aspidistra Flying. Dir. Robert Bierman.
Screenplay by Alan Plater. 1997.
Animal Farm. (TV) Dir. John Stephenson. Screenplay by
Alan Janes and Martyn Burke. 1999.
George Orwell: A Life in Pictures. (TV Documentary).
Dir. Chris Durlacher. Biopic on the life of George
Orwell. Screenplay by Chris Durlacher and Paul
Whittington. 2003.
George Orwell: The South Bank Show. (TV
Documentary). Dir. Leo Burley. Based on the life and
work of George Orwell. Screenplay by D. J. Taylor.
2003.

Notes

Part I, The Life of George Orwell
Chapter 1

p. 11, par. 1, Shelden, Michael, *Orwell: The Authorized Biography,* (New York: Harper Collins, 1992), pp. 14–15.

p. 11, par. 3, Taylor, D. J., *Orwell: The Life* (New York: Henry Holt, 2003), p. 18.

p. 14, par. 2, Shelden, p. 31.

p. 14, par. 3, Qtd. in Shelden, p. 53.

p. 15, par. 1, Taylor, p. 318.

p. 15, par. 2, Davison, Peter, *George Orwell: A Literary Life* (New York: St. Martin's, 1996), pp. 7–8.

p. 15, par. 3, Qtd. in Shelden, p. 71.

p. 18, par. 3, Davison, p. 48.

p. 18, par. 4, Taylor, p. 66.

p. 19, par. 2–p. 20, par. 1, Orwell, George, *Burmese Days* (New York: Harvest, 1974), p. 280.

p. 20, par. 2, Orwell, George, *The Road to Wigan Pier* Chapter 9, http://whitewolf.newcastle.edu.au/words/authors/O/OrwellGeorge/prose/RoadToWiganPier/index.html

p. 20, par. 2, Shelden, p. 131.

p. 21, par. 1, Kerr, Douglas, *George Orwell* (Horndon, UK: Northcote House, 2003), p. 25.

p. 21, par. 2, Mabel Fierz, qtd. in Shelden, p. 135.

p. 21, par. 3, Orwell, George, *The Road to Wigan Pier* (London: Gollancz, 1937), p. 138.

p. 21, par. 5, Sheldon, p. 142.

p. 22, par. 5, Qtd. in Shelden, p. 164.

p. 23, par. 2, Orwell, George, *Down and Out in Paris and London* (New York: Harvest, 1972), p. 115.

p. 23, par. 3, Hammond, J. R., *A George Orwell Chronology* (New York: Palgrave, 2000), p. 19.

p. 24, par. 2, *À la Belle de Nuit.*

p. 24, par. 3, Sheldon, pp. 194–195.

p. 25, par. 2, Mackenzie and Priestley qtd. in Chapter 7 of Bernard Crick's *Orwell: A Life,* http://www.orwell.ru/ a_life/Bernard_Crick/english/

p. 25, par. 2, Gorman, Herman, "On Paris and London Pavements," *New York Times* (Aug. 6, 1933), p. BR4.

p. 26, par. 4, Hammond, p. 30.

p. 26, par. 4, *Times Literary Supplement* (April 11, 1935), p. 245.

p. 26, par. 4, both Quennell and Hartley qtd. in Shelden, p. 246.

p. 26, par. 5–p. 27, par. 1, *Times Literary Supplement* (July 18, 1935), p. 462.

p. 27, par. 2, Qtd. in Shelden, p. 246.

p. 27, par. 3, Shelden, p. 265.

p. 27, par. 4, Davison, p. 67.

p. 29, par. 1, Taylor, p. 177.

p. 29, par. 3, Shelden, p. 273.

p. 29, par. 3, Beadle, Gordon R., "George Orwell's Literary Studies of Poverty in England," *Twentieth Century Literature* 24.2 (1978), p. 189.

p. 29, par. 4, Sturch, Elizabeth L., "The New Novels," *Times Literary Supplement* (May 2, 1936), p. 376.

p. 29, par. 4, Eileen left school before completing her master's degree.

p. 30, par. 1, Wollheim, Richard, "Orwell Reconsidered," *Modern Critical Views: George Orwell,* (New York: Chelsea House, 1987), ed. Harold Bloom, p. 68.

p. 30, par. 1, Shelden, p. 274.

p. 30, par. 1, Orwell, George, *Homage to Catalonia* (New York: Harcourt, 1952), p. 61.

p. 31, par. 1, Orwell, *Homage to Catalonia,* p. 60.

p. 31, par. 2, Orwell, *Homage to Catalonia,* p. 72.

p. 32, par. 3–p. 33, par. 1, Orwell, *Homage to Catalonia*, p. 185.

p. 33, par. 2, Shelden, p. 323.

p. 35, par. 2, Orwell, George, letter to Cyril Connolly (December 14, 1938), *Collected Essays, Journalism and Letters of George Orwell*, Vol. I (London: Secker and Warburg, 1968), ed. Sonia Orwell and Ian Angus.

p. 36, par. 1, Taylor, p. 350.

p. 37, par. 1, Excerpted from publisher's advertising for the series. Qtd. in Shelden, pp. 401–402.

p. 37, par. 4, Shelden, p. 433.

p. 38, par. 3, Shelden, p. 436.

p. 40, par. 5, Shelden, p. 483.

p. 42, par. 3, Qtd. in Shelden, p. 512.

p. 42, par. 3, Prescott, Orville, "Books of the Times," *New York Times* (June 13, 1949), p. 17.

Chapter 2

p. 48, par. 2, Steinhoff, William, *George Orwell and the Origins of 1984* (Ann Arbor: University of Michigan Press, 1975), p. 91.

p. 48, par. 3, Orwell, George, "Marrakech," in *Collected Essays*, p. 388.

Part II, The Writing of George Orwell
Chapter 1

p. 55, par. 1, Frye, Northrup, "Orwell and Marxism," in *George Orwell* (New York: Chelsea House, 1987), ed. Harold Bloom, p. 10.

p. 55, par. 2, James Arnt Aune provides a clear description of *Animal Farm*,'s parallels to history in "Literary Analysis of Animal Farm" in *Understanding Animal Farm* (Westport: Greenwood, 1999), ed. John Rodden.

p. 56, par. 2, all quotations from George Orwell, *Animal Farm* (New York: Signet, 1996).

Chapter 2

p. 85, par. 1, Donoghue, Denis, *Nineteen Eighty-Four*: Politics and Fable," in *George Orwell & Nineteen Eighty-Four: The Man and the Book* (Washington, DC: Library of Congress, 1984), pp. 57–69.

p. 85, par. 2, Fromm, Erich, "Afterword," reprinted in George Orwell, *Nineteen Eighty-Four* (New York: Signet Classic, 1984).

p. 85, par. 3, Read, Herbert, *1984*, in *Modern Critical Views of George Orwell*, ed. Harold Bloom (New York: Chelsea House, 1987), pp. 1.

p. 86, par. 1, Lionel Trilling qtd. in Harold Bloom, "Introduction," in *Modern Critical Views of George Orwell* (New York: Chelsea House, 1987), p. 1.

p. 87, par. 2, Jenni Calder, *Animal Farm* and *Nineteen Eighty-Four* (Philadelphia: Open Univeristy Press, 1987), p. 41.

p. 121, pars. 3–4, *Our Job Is to Make life Worth Living: 1949–1950, The Complete Works of George Orwell*, vol. 20, ed. Peter Davison (London: Secker and Warburg, 1998), p. 136.

Further Information

Further Reading

Bloom, Harold. *George Orwell's* 1984. New York: Chelsea House, 2004.

Brunsdale, Mitzi M. *Student Companion to George Orwell.* New York: Greenwood Press, 2000.

Kerr, Douglas. *George Orwell.* London: Northcote House, 2003.

Lucas, Scott. *Orwell* (Life & Times Series). New York: Haus, 2003.

Rodden, John, ed. *Understanding* Animal Farm: *A Student Casebook to Issues, Sources, and Historical Documents.* Westport, CT: Greenwood, 1999.

Web Sites

The Complete Works of George Orwell
http://www.george-orwell.org

The George Orwell Archive at University College London
http://www.ucl.ac.uk/Library/special-coll/orwell.shtml

Orwell Exhibition Online at Brown University
http://www.brown.edu/Facilities/University_Library/libs
/hay/collections/orwell/leab.html

Resources on History of Socialism at Fordam University
http://www.fordham.edu/halsall/mod/modsbook33.html

Russian Web Site on George Orwell
http://orwell.ru

World Socialist Web Site Page on George Orwell
http://www.wsws.org/news/1998/sep1998/orw-s09.shtml

Bibliography

Beadle, Gordon R, "George Orwell's Literary Studies of Poverty in England." *Twentieth Century Literature* 24.2 (1978): 189.

Bloom, Harold, ed. *Modern Critical Views: George Orwell*. New York: Chelsea House, 1987.

Calder, Jenni. Animal Farm *and* Nineteen Eighty-Four. Philadelphia: Open University Press, 1987, 41.

Crick, Bernard. *Orwell: A Life.* www.orwell.ru, © 1999-2004, http://www.orwell.ru/a_life/Bernard_Crick/english/

Davison, Peter. *George Orwell: A Literary Life.* New York: St. Martin's, 1996, 7–8.

Davison, Peter, ed. *Our Job Is to Make Life Worth Living: 1949–1950, The Complete Works of George Orwell,* vol. 20, London: Secker and Warburg, 1998, 136.

Donoghue, Denis. "*Nineteen Eighty-Four:* Politics and Fable," *George Orwell & Nineteen Eighty-Four: The Man and the Book.* Washington, DC: U.S. Government Printing Office, 1985, 57–69.

Fromm, Erich, "Afterword." Reprinted in George Orwell, *Nineteen Eighty-Four.* New York: Signet Classic, 1984.

Frye, Northrup. "Orwell and Marxism." In Bloom, *George Orwell,* 10.

Gorman, Herman. "On Paris and London Pavements," *New York Times*, August 6, 1933, BR4.

Hammond, J. R. *A George Orwell Chronology*. New York: Palgrave, 2000, 19.

Kerr, Douglas. *George Orwell*. Horndon, UK: Northcote House, 2003, 25.

Orwell, George. *Animal Farm*. New York: Signet, 1996.

———. *Burmese Days*. New York: Harvest, 1974, 280.

———. *Down and Out in Paris and London*. New York: Harvest, 1972, 115.

———. *Homage to Catalonia*. New York: Harcourt, 1952, 61.

———. "Marrakech," in Orwell and Angus, *The Collected Essays*, vol. 1, 388.

———. *The Road to Wigan Pier*. London: Gollancz, 1937, 138.

———. *The Road to Wigan Pier*. University of Newcastle, Australia, http://whitewolf.newcastle.edu.au/words/authors/O/OrwellGeorge/prose/RoadToWiganPier/index.html

Orwell, Sonia, and Ian Angus, eds. *The Collected Essays, Journalism, and Letters of George Orwell*, vol. 1, London: Secker and Warburg, 1968.

Prescott, Orville. "Books of the Times," *New York Times*, June 13, 1949, 17.

Read, Herbert. *1984*. In Bloom, *George Orwell*, 25.

Shelden, Michael. *Orwell: The Authorized Biography*. New York: HarperCollins, 1992, 14–15.

Steinhoff, William. *George Orwell and the Origins of 1984*. Ann Arbor: University of Michigan Press, 1975, 91.

Sturch, Elizabeth L. "The New Novels," *The Times Literary Supplement*, May 2, 1936, 376.

Taylor, D. J. *Orwell: The Life*. New York: Henry Holt, 2003, 18.

Wollheim, Richard. "Orwell Reconsidered." In Bloom, *George Orwell*, 68.

Index

Page numbers in **boldface** are illustrations.
Proper names of fictional characters are shown by (C).

About the Author

Kevin A. Boon is an assistant professor at Penn State University and English Program Coordinator for the Mont Alto campus. He teaches film, writing, and literature, and is the author and editor of a number of books on Kurt Vonnegut, Virginia Woolf, and other writers. He is also an award-winning poet and fiction writer, a skilled composer and musician, and a produced playwright. His most recent book for Marshall Cavendish Benchmark was *Ernest Hemingway: The Sun Also Rises and Other Works*, in this series.